T!...g

D1353054

Teach Yourself®

Thrifty Living
Barty Phillips

For UK order enquiries: please contact Bookpoint Ltd,
130 Milton Park, Abingdon, Oxon OX14 4SB.
Telephone: +44 (0) 1235 827720. Fax: +44 (0) 1235 400454.
Lines are open 09.00–17.00, Monday to Saturday, with a 24-hour
message answering service. Details about our titles and how to
order are available at www.teachyourself.com

For USA order enquiries: please contact McGraw-Hill Customer
Services, PO Box 545, Blacklick, OH 43004-0545, USA.
Telephone: 1-800-722-4726. Fax: 1-614-755-5645.

For Canada order enquiries: please contact McGraw-Hill
Ryerson Ltd, 300 Water St, Whitby, Ontario L1N 9B6, Canada.
Telephone: 905 430 5000. Fax: 905 430 5020.

Long renowned as the authoritative source for self-guided
learning – with more than 50 million copies sold worldwide –
the **Teach Yourself** series includes over 500 titles in the fields of
languages, crafts, hobbies, business, computing and education.

British Library Cataloguing in Publication Data:
a catalogue record for this title is available from the British Library.

Library of Congress Catalog Card Number: on file.

First published in UK 2007 by Hodder Education, part of
Hachette UK, 338 Euston Road, London NW1 3BH.

First published in US 2007 by The McGraw-Hill Companies, Inc.

This edition published 2010.

Previously published as *Teach Yourself Thrifty Living.*

The **Teach Yourself** name is a registered trade mark of
Hodder Headline.

Copyright © 2007, 2010 Barty Phillips

Typeset by MPS Limited, a Macmillan C

Printed in Great Britain for Hodder Edu
Company, 338 Euston Road, London N
Wyman, Reading, Berkshire RG1 8EX.

The publisher has used its best endeavou
for external websites referred to in this b
at the time of going to press. However, t
have no responsibility for the websites ar
that a site will remain live or that the cor
decent or appropriate.

Hachette UK's policy is to use papers tha
and recyclable products and made from
forests. The logging and manufacturing
conform to the environmental regulation

Impression number   10 9 8 7 6

Year   2014 2013

Acknowledgements

Many thanks to all those people who came up with thrifty advice and ideas while I was working on this book, including Sarah Cowley, Mary Cruickshank, Judith Downie, Rom and Eion Downs, Tiffany Foster, Jane Glynn, John Houston, Will Howie, Philip and Christine Mannington, Olivia Mora, Heather Park, Charlie Phillips, Chrissie Phillips, Jane Priestman, Sarah Tisdall, Carole Vincent – and of course that fount of all wisdom, my mother, all those years ago, who taught me the many uses of lemons.

Image credits

Front cover: © Stockbyte/Getty Images

Back cover: © Jakub Semeniuk/iStockphoto.com, © Royalty-Free/Corbis, © agencyby/iStockphoto.com, © Andy Cook/iStockphoto.com, © Christopher Ewing/iStockphoto.com, © zebicho – Fotolia.com, © Geoffrey Holman/iStockphoto.com, © Photodisc/Getty Images, © James C. Pruitt/iStockphoto.com, © Mohamed Saber – Fotolia.com

Contents

Meet the author

Welcome to *Thrifty Living*!

Being thrifty is seldom an inborn gift. Successful thriftiness comes from a combination of common sense, experience and listening to the experts. My own thriftiness, such as it is, was probably born in the years immediately after World War II when one pat of butter had to last a week and you saved up coupons to buy enough cotton to make a new blouse for the summer. Later, as a young mother I learned to juggle the rent arrears with the housekeeping budget, to make home-made soup last a very long time and to eke out my weekly child allowance so we all had enough to eat.

I am lucky enough to rather enjoy the challenge of managing to afford the things I like without getting into debt. In times of hardship or recession, being thrifty becomes an absolute necessity. This book introduces readers to the pleasures and satisfactions of being thrifty and also to the fact that we can't all be automatically thrifty in all aspects of our lives. We need the experts too especially where investments or debts are concerned.

Barty Phillips

Only got a minute?

Thrifty living means working out a way of living within our means instead of continually owing money through our credit, debit and store cards. This is particularly important in times of economic difficulty when we need to conserve our basic resources. To live more thriftily you should:

▶ Use less oil, gas and electricity and keep warm by wearing more clothes and taking more exercise.

▶ Learn to control your money rather than letting your money control you.

▶ Shop less but more thoughtfully.

▶ Spend some of your holidays locally to save on the cost of travel and hotels.

▶ Use public transport, a bike or your legs instead of always climbing into the car.

▶ Cook your own meals rather than relying on ready-meals from the freezer or pizza takeaways.

Thrifty living doesn't have to mean giving up the good things in life. It does mean thinking twice about how you spend your money and being creative in your spending.

5 Only got five minutes?

Spendthrift pitfalls

Most people in the Western world are permanently in debt without even realizing it. We pay for things with credit cards, store cards, debit cards and pay off the minimum amount allowed each month. Most of us have no idea how much we owe on these cards at any one time. There is nothing to fall back on and no way to pay off the mortgage should you lose your job or have to take a cut in salary.

Because credit is so easy to come by, we simply don't realize how much we are spending on completely unnecessary luxuries: anything from using the car when walking or biking would get us there just as quickly, not bothering to turn off lights when moving from one room to another; paying for holidays on credit and spending the rest of the year paying for what we've already enjoyed.

Because it's so easy, we don't sit down and work out a realistic budget but just imagine we're living within our means. And there are plenty of other ways in which we throw our money away. We are careless shoppers, easily tempted and ready to buy on impulse. We don't nearly often enough ask ourselves whether we need a thing, ask the right questions about fitness for purpose – for example: how much electricity will your new washing machine use? Is your new jacket machine washable? Will your new car qualify for a reduced registration fee or have you set your heart on a four-wheel drive macho-machine?

Everyday shopping is one of the ways in which we can be successfully thrifty with immediate and obvious results.

For example, with supermarket shelves piled high with amazingly tempting variety it's so very easy to spend money like water on food, to go home with twice as much as we need, much of which will be thrown away at the end of the week because we haven't got around to eating it.

We are inveterate shoppers but not thrifty shoppers. We don't learn about our rights as consumers, we don't research expensive products properly although the information exists and is not difficult to find; we buy on impulse and not on information received.

We are even worse when buying online, snapping up one-click bargains without a moment's thought although it only needs two or three such purchases to find we can't afford to pay the next garage or electricity bill. That is not thrifty living.

One mistake made by many of us is to ignore any offers, grants, subsidies and special deals that may be on offer. Paying by card is so easy, so quick, so tempting – why go to the bother of collecting up tokens and using them on time, filling in boring forms for local authority grants towards insulation, or other ecological improvements?

Thrifty budgeting would soon tell us that the trouble taken to use such offers efficiently could soon save enough money to pay for a holiday abroad or a wind turbine on the roof.

Learn to live thriftily and let thrifty living become as natural as cleaning your teeth.

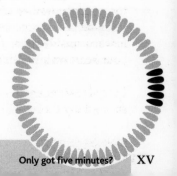

10 Only got ten minutes?

Thrifty strategies

We can take control of our spending and stop the see-saw of surplus and debit, euphoria and worry without losing the quality of our lives. If we are prepared to put real effort into it, it can be satisfying and extremely rewarding.

Some of the most basic thrifty actions will automatically contribute to the conservation of energy, plants and creatures of our planet. They will contribute to the wellbeing of the poor, the hungry and the displaced of the world. So being thrifty in personal ways helps us to be thrifty in a much larger arena.

Saving money

▶ We need to put aside some money regularly. It doesn't matter how well-off you are or how much money you earn, if you are thrifty you will put money aside for unforeseen circumstances, so you can always pay the mortgage, always feed the family and, when the time comes, rely on a satisfactory pension for your later years.

▶ If you don't have enough to invest, put a regular amount into a savings account to accrue interest. The more you save, the more you will accrue and as time goes by this can amount to a surprisingly generous amount. Make this an untouchable account so it really can grow. It can be heartwarming to organize this buffer against hard times.

Budgeting

- ▶ Make a list of money coming into your account and money going out.
- ▶ Put aside what you need for household bills and other essentials, including savings – anything left is there to spend. Don't cheat.
- ▶ If you receive your income weekly, keep a weekly budget. If you are paid monthly, sit down on the first of every month and do your sums.
- ▶ Keep a spreadsheet or a separate book for your accounts so you can refer back to past months and years at a glance.

Shop wisely

- ▶ Food shopping can be highly wasteful, so make a list of what you really need, enjoy choosing the things on the list but don't keep throwing extras that you don't need into your trolley. Try to buy only enough so you won't eventually have to throw good food away.
- ▶ Save money on clothes by buying in sales, holding on to existing clothes a bit longer and accessorizing rather than buying a new wardrobe every season. A new scarf, leggings or beaded bag can be as effective and confidence-boosting as yet another black suit.
- ▶ Internet shopping makes it easy to compare prices so do it, especially when you want to buy something costly.

Thrifty leisure time

- ▶ If your budget doesn't allow for eating out every evening, look for cheaper ways of being entertained. Keep your eyes open for special deals at restaurants, cheap evenings at cinemas,

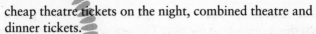

cheap theatre tickets on the night, combined theatre and dinner tickets.

▶ Investigate the possibilities of discounts for early booking on public transport and always ask if you qualify for concessionary tickets.

▶ Set aside a fund for your holidays and don't pay for them on credit. Then you won't be paying for last year's holiday long after it's all over.

Reuse and recycle

▶ Don't buy over-packaged goods and be prepared to leave unnecessary packaging in the supermarket.

▶ Many supermarket containers are excellent for freezing soups and sauces you make at home – why buy new containers if you don't need to?

▶ Books, clothes and other items that clutter up your home are welcomed by charity shops, which can in themselves provide thrifty answers to household requirements.

Ten ways to save money now

Here are ten ways in which you can begin saving money immediately. Most of them are easy, all are encouraging, none needs much unusual equipment or preparation and each will help set you firmly on the road to thrifty living. The savings for a year on each of these simple frugal decisions can be surprising.

1 **Drink tap water**
   Fill a mineral water bottle with water from the tap to carry with you for the day.
   If you drink 1.5 litres of water daily – the recommended amount for adults – why pay for mineral water when you can get tap water practically free? If you don't like the taste, add

a squeeze of lemon juice or a couple of mint leaves to give it a fresh, thirst-quenching flavour. This not only saves on the cost of water but also on the use of plastic bottles, thus offering the double advantage of helping the environment. Saving: around £700 ($1,050).

2   Take a packed lunch to work
A soup-and-roll lunch with a cappuccino to follow in a local café may seem a cheap way to eat during the day but if you reckon how much that daily meal has cost, you will find it could be enough to have paid for a summer holiday. A home-made packed lunch of a sandwich, an apple, a small chocolate bar and a bottle of tap water could help you pay for that holiday. Saving: around £700 ($1,050).

3   Redeem all the vouchers languishing in your purse
Go straight out and use all those vouchers you have received from stores and garden centres before they pass their redeem-by date. Individually they may not amount to much but if you manage to use them all over a year you could save substantially. Savings: perhaps £200 ($300).

4   Give up smoking
So much smoking these days has to take place in the street, huddled in a doorway – there has never been a better time to give up. Not only will it make you feel better, but food will taste better, everything will smell better, including your clothes, and if you smoke around 20 cigarettes a day, giving up could save £2,000 ($3,000) a year.

5   Give up your store cards
Cut up all your store cards and go for a walk at your lunch break instead of going to the shops. Store cards entice customers with offers of ten per cent discount on goods but don't forget they can charge up to 30 per cent interest so you are losing and they're gaining on every item that you buy with them. Savings: incalculable.

6 Walk to work/the station/your bus stop

Get up half an hour earlier each morning and give yourself time to eat breakfast and then walk. This will wake you up, tone the muscles and save on bus or train fares or the costs of driving to work. Depending on your usual method of transport and how far you have to go, this could save you around £100 ($150) a month.

7 Make use of free daily papers on the way to work

Don't buy a regular newspaper every day. Pick up a free paper in which you'll get the news, the cartoons, the crosswords just the same as in your usual paper and then you can leave it on the bus or train when you've finished with it for the next person to read and there's no searching round for a recycling bin. Saving: £142 ($213) a year.

8 Switch off your electrical equipment

Before going out for the day or going to bed at night, switch off all your electrical equipment and appliances. All the bright little lights, the clock on your microwave oven, the computer monitor are using electricity. Savings: incalculable but substantial.

9 Lengthen the life of your child's felt pens

Open up the back of any felt pen that has dried out and pour a drop or two of vinegar into the tube. Put back the stopper and shake the pen a little. The colour will magically return. This little addition of vinegar can make pens last twice as long, particularly as children so often forget to put the tops back on properly. Savings: perhaps £5 ($7.50).

10 Make use of your local library

Visit the library and borrow some books or CDs or DVDs. Borrowing library books is a real bargain and not just for novels but for travel information, practical information and, of course, music and films. The library has the advantage of free newspapers and magazines that you can sit and read at leisure. What's more you can stay there pretty well all day in warmth and comfort. Savings, if you're a fast reader: around £300 ($450).

Introduction

Some are born thrifty some achieve thriftiness and some have thriftiness thrust upon them.

With apologies to Shakespeare

Thrifty living can become a fascinating way of life. The thrifty person learns to look out for opportunities to save money at home, at work, at play and while travelling, relaxing and shopping. As you become more skilled at being thrifty, there is enormous satisfaction, not just in the savings made, but in the ability to spot and exploit the opportunities.

Thrifty living can mean substantial savings so that even on a meagre budget, you can still afford the odd luxury. It can allow you to live comfortably within constrained means, rather than struggling from day to day with a hand-to-mouth existence. As a beneficial side effect, being thrifty is also environmentally friendly, encouraging the saving of resources and recycling of materials.

Thrifty strategies may be as mundane as dealing regularly with household bills, as pleasant as spending a day in the local library (free warmth, seating and reading), as creative as making your own Christmas cards or as simple as taking your own packed lunch to work.

Who should read this book?

Almost everybody could benefit from reading this book. Anyone on a tight budget can make substantial savings by learning its lessons. For example, elderly and retired people living on pensions, who are not as well off as they once were; students struggling to make ends meet; parents with offspring of any age, who have dozens of calls on their income until the children finish their education;

high-earning young professionals with no personal commitments who find they are suddenly in debt through credit card overspending. All these people will find invaluable suggestions here. Some will want to monitor and record their successes and savings. Others will simply want to follow the ideas and guidelines and reap the benefits in a less formal way. In any event, thrifty living can be both satisfying and fruitful at one level and, if nothing else, prevent you from getting into serious financial trouble.

How to use this book

This book can be used in a number of ways. You could work your way through each chapter, learning the skills of thrifty living in a dedicated and formalized way, rather like working your way through a structured college course. Or you can dip into the chapters that you feel concern you most at any particular time and benefit from the advice and guidelines on one particular area of thrifty expertise.

As with all learning, you will not suddenly become much better off simply through reading the information. You will need to understand and absorb the principles behind the guidelines before you can suit them to your particular circumstances. And understanding them is not enough – you have to actually practise them, so have patience.

The book starts with the principles of thrift and some of the background information you need to know before you begin. Remember that frugal living is largely a matter of common sense, but it is sometimes difficult to resist the endless seductive invitations to part with money, borrow it, invest it, buy with it or, often, simply throw it away. As a result, the first principles are to arm oneself against such invitations, to learn to pause, consider and test the water before plunging in. Read each chapter paragraph by paragraph and try the quick test at the end of each one. If you can't answer every question, try going through the chapter again.

The information includes general guidance on acquiring thrifty habits, some facts on your shopping rights, advice on borrowing and investing, how to save on household bills, and on shopping generally, using the internet, recycling, economies at home, on holiday, during leisure time and even in the garden. There are also some pointers on ways in which you can add a little to your income. Use this book to help you become thrifty in whatever aspect of your life you wish and to become confident and secure when dealing with money.

Finally, always remember the thrifty rule where spending money is concerned: if in doubt – don't.

1

....

Getting the thrifty habit

In this chapter you will learn:
* *reasons for being thrifty*
* *how to think thriftily*
* *how to incorporate thrift into daily life.*

Reasons for being thrifty

We live in an age of extraordinary luxury. Fresh food of all seasons and from all corners of the earth is piled high on supermarket shelves, in corner shops and on market stalls. Clothes, jewellery, crafts and objets d'art cry out to be bought from beautifully designed displays in expensive galleries. Holidays in the sun, in rented villas or in adventurous situations are available and costly. Music – as much as anyone could want to listen to in a lifetime – can be downloaded into a tiny personal iPod. Money itself is available at the swipe of a small plastic card even in the remotest of areas. Easy credit is available at the drop of a hat making all these myriad temptations so desirable. Living expenses meanwhile rise inexorably. There is probably a mortgage to keep up, various insurances to buy, utilities, education, credit card and car expenses to cater for.

The temptations and the sheer choice of what we can have or do, the fact that the cost of everything seems to keep rising all the time and the terrifying thought that with so much on offer one might actually miss out on something means that most people live in debt. Some are in debt even though earning good salaries because they spend to their limit, thinking the money can be paid off at any moment. Others are in debt because their earnings or pensions are too small to actually cover the cost of living. Either way life is underlined by a constant, often hidden, thread of anxiety about money. There is a pattern of spend and worry, spend and worry and by degrees debts are built up which are difficult to pay off. The alternative seems to be to live miserably, keeping within means that don't seem adequate. The result is uncomfortable, anxious-making and sometimes downright frightening.

People living on very small pensions or grants learn to live economically and when the money runs out halfway through the week, they simply 'sit and wait' hungrily for pension day to come round. Mr Micawber in Charles Dickens' *David Copperfield* put it nicely: 'Annual income twenty pounds, annual expenditure nineteen pounds nineteen and six, result happiness. Annual income twenty pounds, annual expenditure twenty pounds ought and six, result misery.' You have to remember that there were 20 shillings in the pound at that time, but it was that crucial sixpence that made the difference. Whether you are a student with a loan and books to buy, a young parent with a small brood of young to rear, an established entrepreneur with a business to run or a pensioner trying to make do on much less than you are accustomed to, getting into debt is an expensive business and getting out of debt can seem like an impossibility.

Not getting into debt in the first place is a good goal. Remember that many things that sound like bargains are certainly not.

Obvious examples include the free glass of wine you get when you hire a personal shopper; or indeed, the personal shopper him/herself. Will you feel obliged to buy more than you really can afford? Another example is the tempting 'cheap' timeshare somewhere in the sun where you are never free to take the two weeks scheduled for your use and which has no resale value. On a more basic level, buying lashings of expensive luxuries from the supermarket is a quick way of getting into debt which can be avoided with just a small amount of foresight and planning.

Insight

Add up all purchases made using your credit cards every month so you know exactly how much you owe. The actual sum can give you a salutary fright.

Thrift as a way of life

This is where thrift, that quaint old concept, comes into its own. Thrift is the skill of managing your money, whether much or little, so that you can live a satisfying life without getting into debt. The purpose of thrift is not to give yourself a reduced lifestyle but by regularly and consistently saving unnecessary expenditure as a matter of course, to achieve particular goals. Your goals initially might be simply to limit your debts. If you could reduce your long-term borrowings, for example, just to your house mortgage, wouldn't that release your mind from anxiety and your money for planned luxuries, large or small? Successful thrift needs to be practised every day, as naturally as brushing your teeth or checking your emails. It needs to be approached with determination and enthusiasm, to become part of the fabric of everyday life. It's not the sudden occasional discovery of an unexpected bargain. It's a question of systematically getting into the habit of considering every purchase you make day to day, planning important purchases ahead of time, researching the possibilities and dangers of every investment you plan to make and being generally aware of how much money you actually have to spend.

Most people are in debt not because there is not enough money coming in, but because the money is dribbling away in tiny droplets which seem insignificant when taken individually but amount to a horrendous sum when added up. Limiting mad splurges on expensive treats or luxury holidays to far parts of the world is an obvious way of providing the wherewithal to pay off debts. Thrift should not become a burden; it should be approached with a sense of adventure and achievement. The aim is certainly not to lose out on fun and good experiences but to relieve you of the anxiety of debt and conserve your money for things you really want.

The following strategies all appear in greater detail in later chapters of this book but it is wise to include the headings in your day-to-day thrift plan so that you can make sure you are including the essentials.

Day-to-day ways of being thrifty

Day-to-day expenditure on smaller luxuries can actually amount to almost as much as the seemingly larger splurges. Why spend a packet on congratulatory or consoling flowers when you could pay half that much for a cheaper version or even make a posy from your own garden that would give just as much pleasure? (Bouquets of flowers laid at the site of an accident are often not even taken out of their wrappings. How much of a waste is that?)

Why spend on new books when you could find the same books in a second-hand bookshop or on Amazon for half the price? Why buy expensive fizzy drinks to pop in the fridge for your children when tap water is better for them? Children brought up to drink water often prefer it to over-sweet drinks anyway.

Insight
Home-made soups are among the cheapest and most delicious meals you can eat. Make a lot, eat half and freeze half in old supermarket soup cartons – defrost in the microwave, saving electricity.

Another way to save money is to be more creative at home. There is huge satisfaction in creating home-made greetings cards, altering clothes, recycling cardboard and generally beating the mountains of spendaholic clutter that gathers around us with all its accompanying guilt. For example, why get a store to alter the hem on your new trousers when it only takes half an hour or so to do it yourself? Why throw away old egg boxes when they make such great little seed trays for propagating tomatoes? They can even be used to make papier maché for bowls or ornaments or simply add organic matter to the compost heap.

DOWN WITH THE JONESES

It can be difficult, when you see friends and neighbours investing in expensive luxuries – a new family transporter say, or a grand new conservatory tacked on to the house – not to feel envious or diminished. This is where you should train yourself to be proud of your eco-friendlier small engine car and wear it as a badge of honour. Be purposefully a little eccentric in your approach to life, make some mileage out of being intentionally and successfully thrifty. Where clothes are concerned, you only need a few, well-chosen garments that you really enjoy wearing which can be dressed up with a variety of accessories like scarves or unusual jewellery. Don't put your friends down by seeming to be more 'worthy' than they are but enjoy the pleasure and fun you get out of making alternative decisions.

Children at school can encounter real difficulties where their peer groups are concerned. If all your children's friends can buy loads of crisps and chocolate bars during the lunch break, how can you encourage your children to buy an apple or a bunch of grapes instead? If their friends are given expensive birthday parties with bought-in entertainment and to-die-for presents, how do you avoid doing the same? Alternative solutions may take some ingenuity but it's sometimes possible to make a pact with other parents to provide particular packed lunches or to invite fewer children to the cinema or a meal at the local pizza house instead of committing to huge parties.

TAKE NOTES

First of all, get into the habit of taking notes, comparing prices and balancing the advantages against the disadvantages of particular transactions you are considering.

Carry a notebook, pen and calculator with you wherever you go or record information on your mobile phone and then transfer it to somewhere more permanent. Note what you paid the plumber for renewing washers on the taps; what you paid for the weekly grocery shop; how much a new dress cost; what you paid for the holiday cottage in July and how much it would have cost in February. These notes should encompass everything you do that involves money.

KEEP RECORDS

When you get home transfer the information in your notebook into a simple filing system so that you can check on it when you need to at a later date. It doesn't matter whether your filing system is on your computer, in box or in envelope files, or even in a diary as long as you know where to get at it and remember to use it.

Insight

Your mobile phone can take the place of an old-fashioned notebook, provided you keep it in good order and well organized. You must know how to find the information you need later.

THINK BEFORE YOU BUY

Never buy in a hurry. Thrift is as much about planning as about not spending. Even with a comparatively small purchase like a clock radio or a dress, give yourself time to consider first of all whether it's actually the one you want and secondly whether you need it at all. Don't buy anything just because it's cheap. Small impulse buys are often disastrous. That nifty little dress you happen to see, looking really attractive in a shop window or on an internet site so often turns out to be a disappointment – when you get it home you find it doesn't quite fit and anyway red has never suited you. When faced with impulse buys like this, it's best to walk out of the shop or turn off the computer with the intention of perhaps going back to have another look later – with any luck you will be able to congratulate yourself that you forgot or didn't have time.

DO YOUR RESEARCH

Protect yourself against bad buys and bad bargains. If you are making a big purchase like a new car, for example, deciding what you want for your money will involve decisions about petrol consumption, interior layout, the ergonomics of the seating, safety considerations, where you can get the vehicle serviced and how easy it will be to get parts. You really need time to think these things through carefully and if possible, discuss them with somebody else to get an objective viewpoint.

Insight

Price comparison websites can be helpful when doing your research, giving you an instant insight into what you can expect to pay for a particular item.

Read specialist magazines, join consumer organizations, look up the subject online (but remember opinions on the web are often subjective and not always to be relied on). Visit specialist stores, examine the merchandise and ask questions.

KNOW THE LAW ABOUT CONSUMER SHOPPING

The obvious first call for using your thrift skills is in shopping. Keep a weather-eye out for bargains but buy only what's on your essential or long-term list. There are laws to protect consumers so make sure you know what they are in your country or state and how to use them. In the UK, consumer rights and responsibilities are clear and include trading standards, faulty goods, scams and illegal street trading. There is advice on buying cars, mobile phones, extended warranties and hiring builders and decorators. Any law that applies to shopping 'in the high street' also applies to shopping online. In the USA, there are agencies in every state that can clarify and help with legal problems to do with purchasing goods directly, by phone or online.

BE ON THE ALERT

A purchase made on the spur of the moment can be a disastrous white elephant unless it's something that has been on your 'wanted' list for some time, such as a particular model of a radio or other desired object. You might discover a remaindered lot of your favourite out-of-production T-shirt or the perfect next Christmas present for your husband in January. Remember that a bargain is not a bargain if you buy something, even at the lowest price, that you can't use or don't want and that you can't bring yourself to give away either. Look for out-of-season bargains: holidays outside the school holiday months; summer resort holidays in winter; bikinis in January.

LEARN TO NEGOTIATE

Insight

Remember that bargaining is traditionally not about 'getting the better' of the other person, but about coming to a mutually acceptable price. Both parties should be satisfied at the end.

Bargaining or haggling does not always come naturally to westerners where so many goods are bought in department stores and already marked with prices that seem unalterable. However, haggling is a respected skill in many other countries and something that can be learned for when one is on holiday visiting markets or even on occasions at home. Many people are embarrassed to haggle but that's largely because they are inexperienced. Learn the haggling skill – it's only a form of negotiation – you'll find it's entertaining, rewarding and sociable too.

There are other opportunities for negotiating as well. For example, if goods are slightly damaged you might be able to negotiate a drop in the price. If you offer to buy two or three of something, you might be able to negotiate a special price, rather like bookshops' 'three-for-two' offers (though remember, that's only a bargain if you actually want all three books and haven't already read two of them).

BE MISERLY ABOUT HOUSEHOLD BILLS

There are many ways of saving on electricity and gas in the home and a surprising amount of money to be saved. You can make big savings by buying and using low voltage light bulbs and you can add to your electricity bill alarmingly by leaving light bulbs on or appliances on standby rather than turning them off. Make sure the rest of the household are aware of this too. 'Were you born in a barn?' was a cry in the last century to people who left doors open – letting in cold draughts and letting precious warm air escape. In centrally heated homes it is easy to be unaware of how much electricity is 'leaking' out simply because we can't be bothered to turn things off.

USE YOUR COMPUTER WISELY

From buying the right computer to accessing free games and recognizing good deals on the internet, making the most of competitions and researching special subjects, going online can be extravagant or thrifty depending on how you use it. Going on broadband and communicating by email rather than telephone already constitutes a sizeable saving if you need to contact people frequently.

Insight

Save up your heavy coins in a jar so they don't weigh down your purse. One year's worth of copper coins can amount to a dinner out or something worth adding to your savings account.

You can open a high-interest savings account or, more riskily, invest your money in stocks and shares but don't despise the humble piggy bank. Put in all loose coins or the cash you have not spent on something you thought you wanted. There are piggy banks you cannot get into unless you break them, ensuring that you'll build up a good sum before you broach them. This is an excellent way for children to save for something yearned for. But it is also a good way for adults to save for a particular item such as a new sofa. If you're saving for a new bed for the spare room, you could get your visitors to contribute as well. Savings of small coins build up quickly and can end up as substantial sums which only need a small top up to enable you to buy the object of your dreams.

THRIFT AT HOME

Recycling is not just the thrifty answer to household rubbish but essential thinking for our planet and, crucially, for our children. There are many, many ways of dealing with your waste, from responsible chucking out to creative reuse. Keeping old greetings and postcards in a box with felt pens, adhesive and coloured papers is an immediate invitation to turn them into new cards or gift tags among other things. It's a good way of keeping children absorbed during the holidays – and away from the temptations of shopping. Getting about, to the office or to school or down to the supermarket, offers lots of thrifty opportunities as well, from walking to bicycling or taking the bus.

10 THRIFTY DAY-TO-DAY HINTS AND TIPS

1 *Encourage your children to be thrifty. Give them a modest amount of pocket money each week and let them learn to make the money work for them. Some will save and some will spend but it's all good experience.*

2 *Plan your budget for the week, month or even the year (if you can be that disciplined) and write down your daily expenses so that you can check that you are sticking to it. If you know you've overspent in the first few days, you must cut back for the rest of the week. If you've managed very well in the beginning, you will then be able to buy small treats to make up for it.*

3 *Avoid being mean and stingy; instead, be creative and imaginative – thrift should be an art not a vice.*

4 *Don't get hooked on lotteries. If you fancy the odd flutter, decide how much you are willing to spend each week or month and don't go over that amount – consider it money you are willing to throw away. If you win, that's a bonus.*

5 *If you do splurge on something, make economies elsewhere to balance the budget.*

6 *Make a pact with the parents of your child's best friend to limit expenditure on expensive treats for the kids.*

7 *Buy food in season: strawberries are cheaper and taste better when they haven't been flown halfway round the world and are much more special when you only get them once a year.*

8 *Don't carry more money around with you than you actually need for the day and leave your credit cards behind too. That will make buying on impulse much more difficult.*

9 *Think before you buy. Give yourself time to consider –*
   and then say no.

10 *Learn to negotiate for a discount if goods are slightly damaged*
   or if you are willing to buy in bulk (three for the price of two,
   for example).

QUICK REVISION TEST

1 *What are the purposes of being thrifty?*

2 *Name six ways in which you can be thrifty in one day.*

3 *In what ways can you research an expensive product you would like to purchase?*

4 *What are the thriftiest ways to save money?*

5 *What is the most important rule about debt?*

2

Know your shopping rights

In this chapter you will learn:
- *what laws exist to protect you*
- *when you are entitled to compensation*
- *how to complain.*

How often have you bought something expensive and complicated, such as a washing machine that turned out to be not quite as it was described to you? Perhaps it leaked when it started washing or made noise like a cement mixer when it came to the spin cycle. What do you do when this sort of thing happens, grin and bear it or immediately contact the shop and ask for your money back? They will probably say they can't oblige, it's not in the agreement, so you find you have spent a large amount of money and are stuck with an unsatisfactory item.

But don't be fobbed off so easily. When you buy any object from a shop or store you do have a number of rights controlled by law. As a thrifty expert, it is important that you should know your rights and the many legal safeguards for shoppers that exist. Knowing and understanding these will give you the confidence to make sure you benefit from them and prevent you from being financially worse off after a bad purchase.

Of course, the truly thrifty person will take time over important shopping decisions, research the item desired and buy the right object at the right price without being bullied into buying unsuitable objects. If you have to resort to refunds, compensation or the courts, you have already made thrifty errors. However, even the most thrifty person can make a mistake, so knowing how to rectify bad shopping decisions can be important.

Avoid going to the law if possible. It is expensive and difficult. Even the small claims court can't enforce its judgements without costing you more in the end. Consumers in the UK are particularly well protected. Consumer law in the USA may vary from state to state so get advice from your local consumer organization.

Insight

Where do you keep correspondence about purchases made? Can you find it when you need it? An A4 box file takes up very little space, but is large enough to find easily when necessary.

UK laws to protect consumers

The most important law protecting consumers is the Sale of Goods Act which applies to England, Wales and Northern Ireland but not to Scotland, which has similar but different laws. Under the Sale of Goods Act 1979, goods must be 'as described' and 'of satisfactory quality'. If you discover that something you've bought does not meet these requirements you can reject it and ask for your money back providing you do so quickly. Alternatively, you can request a repair or replacement or claim compensation.

THE SALE OF GOODS ACT

Insight

Read this section through thoroughly and make sure you've grasped the basic points. You will find it invaluable if there's a problem with a purchase – it's better to know your rights in advance.

Under this Act all goods bought by a customer must conform to three things.

1 *They must be of satisfactory quality: this means that the goods must meet the standards that any reasonable person would expect, taking into account the description, the price and all other relevant information. In some circumstances, the retailer may be liable for any statement made by the manufacturer about the goods. Satisfactory quality includes the appearance and finish of the goods, their safety and durability and whether they are free from defects (including minor faults).*

2 *They must be fit for purpose: the goods must be fit for the purpose that such goods are generally sold for (such as a vacuum cleaner for cleaning floors) or suitable for any specific or particular purpose specified at the time of the purchase (such as whether the vacuum will suck up water as well as dust).*

3 *They must be as described: goods should correspond with any description applied to them (for example, something described as made of wood should not turn out to be made of plastic).*

This means that whatever you buy must do what it is supposed to, must be in good condition, free of faults, be safe and must last for a reasonable length of time. The Act gives you six years from the time you buy something to make a claim. But these rights don't extend to an immediate refund for all that time. You only have a relatively short period to get a full refund, after which it is assumed that you have 'accepted' the item.

The Act does not state how long appliances should last but a reasonable lifespan for irons, kettles, hair dryers and other small appliances is 2–5 years; refrigerators, freezers, spin dryers, tumble dryers, microwave ovens, 3–8 years; dishwashers and washing machines should last for 4–8 years; higher priced VCRs and DVDs, 2–5 years; lower priced hi-fi systems, 2–5 years and higher priced hi-fi systems, 5–8 years.

GETTING LEGAL HELP

You can get free legal advice from trading standards officers through your local council or your local Citizens Advice Bureau and you might be lucky enough to have a local authority law centre near you. Many solicitors offer half an hour free legal advice but this may tempt you into getting more help, for which you will have to pay and if you do win, your winnings may disappear into the lawyer's account.

Your household insurance policy may include free legal advice on specific problems. Some unions or trade associations have a free lawyer (the smaller organizations are often the most helpful). Avoid 'no-win no-fee' offers. Solicitors are expensive; you pay for every minute of their time so have all the facts and figures to hand and don't waste time chatting about the weather. Don't get them to write on your behalf; it's cheaper to write your own letter based on what they advise so take notes while they talk. Add 'without prejudice' at the top of your letter then what you say can't be held against you.

WHEN ARE YOU ENTITLED TO COMPENSATION?

If the goods are not of satisfactory quality or are faulty when you buy them, you are legally entitled to ask for a full refund, repair or replacement or a reduction in price.

You should be able to get a full refund if they don't comply with the above laws and if you haven't used or tampered with them in any way and if you take them back promptly.

Insight
If you can, avoid confrontation. Politeness often gets you further than aggression. But if you are confident that you are in the right, be (politely) firm.

'ACCEPTED' GOODS

You will not be able to get a full refund if you have already 'accepted' the goods. That is to say, if you tell the retailer you accept the goods, if you alter or customize the goods in any way or if you keep them for an unreasonable time without telling the seller you have rejected them, you will not be able to get a refund. Once you have accepted the goods, only the following solutions are available:

▸ *Compensation (damages): the amount of compensation (if any) may be based on the cost of repair or if that's not possible, compensation may be based on the purchase price with an allowance for usage.*

▸ *Repair or replacement: the trader can refuse to repair or replace an item if it is disproportionate in comparison to the other solutions. For example, if you ask a trader to replace a washing machine, he would be entitled to turn down your request and offer a repair instead. However, the repair or replacement must be carried out within a reasonable time and without causing significant inconvenience to you. If this does not happen or the repair or replacement is not possible, you can then claim a refund or request a reduction in the purchase price. Ultimately, if a remedy cannot be agreed on and you go to court, the court has the power to choose any of the above solutions.*

> NOTE: These solutions do not apply to hire purchase contracts although other laws apply to them. Contact your local Trading Standards Service for advice.

PROVING THAT SOMETHING IS FAULTY

If you reject the goods and are claiming a full refund or damages, it is YOU, the consumer, who needs to prove that the goods are not of satisfactory quality, fit for purpose or as described at the time of purchase.

If you are claiming repair or replacement within the first six months after purchase, it is for THE TRADER to prove that the goods conformed to the contract when you bought them.

If you are claiming repair or replacement more than six months after purchase, the burden of proof is back to YOU, the consumer.

If it becomes necessary to obtain an expert opinion to support your claim, there are procedures to be followed before you employ anyone in this capacity. County Court rules say that where an expert is necessary, it should be a single, jointly approved expert, and the expert's duty is to the court. You need to agree your choice of expert with the other party, and allow them to put their comments to the expert. Failure to follow this procedure may mean that a judge may not allow your expert to be heard should the matter eventually reach County Court. Your local Trading Standards Service can advise.

Insight

Remember that sometimes it's better to accept a situation than fight through the courts a case you may lose and that, even if you win, will take up precious time, energy and emotion.

WHEN YOU ARE NOT ENTITLED TO ANYTHING

You will not be entitled to anything once you have bought the goods:

▶ *if you were told of any faults before you bought them*
▶ *if the fault was obvious and it would have been reasonable to have noticed it when you examined it before buying*
▶ *if you caused any damage yourself*
▶ *if you made a mistake (e.g. decided you didn't like the colour)*
▶ *if you change your mind about the goods or see them cheaper elsewhere.*

The situation may be different and you may have additional rights where contracts involve credit or distance selling (e.g. internet sales, catalogue or telephone sales).

WHO SHOULD YOU CLAIM AGAINST?

Your claim could be against the retailer under the Sale of Goods Act; the manufacturer (under the terms of a guarantee if you have one); a credit company if financed by credit. If you want to take a claim to court, don't wait too long. The action has to be started within six years of when you bought the item or took delivery (five years in Scotland).

Insight

Be warned, claiming can be time-consuming, annoying and may fail. Weigh up the pros and cons. You may feel it better to treat a bad buy as a useful experience. If you do want to claim, get professional advice, preferably from an objective source.

GUARANTEES

If the manufacturer provides a free guarantee with the goods, then it is his obligation to provide recompense. If the manufacturer fails to honour the guarantee, you could sue for the promises made. A guarantee is extra to your rights under the Sale of Goods Act.

RETURNS POLICIES

Some retailers make promises out of goodwill that they will issue refunds for unused goods within a time period, for whatever reason. This creates additional useful rights for the consumer.

EXTRA SAFEGUARDS FOR ELECTRICAL AND GAS APPLIANCES

As with all other goods, electrical and gas appliances must be of satisfactory quality, fit for purpose and as described. If you are dissatisfied with the goods here's what you should do:

▶ *If you've used the item only a few times or haven't had a reasonable opportunity to check it, you are probably entitled to a refund for a fault or poor description or you may request a replacement.*
▶ *If the fault is only minor and can easily be put right it is reasonable to accept a repair. This won't stop you from claiming a replacement or refund if the repair turns out to be unsatisfactory.*

> ▶ *If you have used it more than a few times or have had a reasonable opportunity to check it, you are probably still entitled to a repair or replacement. A repair should be carried out within a reasonable period of time and without causing you significant inconvenience. Any repair should restore goods to a satisfactory condition. If this does not happen, you are entitled to a replacement or compensation. This could be a sum of money or the cost of hiring a temporary replacement or perhaps the loan of a replacement.*

> ▶ *If the goods cannot be replaced or repaired economically, you are entitled to a refund. The trader may make a reduction from the price you paid to allow for the use you have had from the goods.*

> ▶ *If the goods have damaged anything or cost you money in any other way, you may be entitled to extra compensation.*

NOTE: It is the trader who must sort out your problem, not the manufacturer.

SOME PROBLEM AREAS

Private sales
When you buy goods from a private individual, you don't have the same rights as when buying from a trader. The legal principle of caveat emptor or 'buyer beware' operates here. You have no rights to expect that goods be of satisfactory quality or fit for their purpose, but there is a requirement that they should be 'as described'. You should check goods thoroughly before you buy them.

Second-hand goods
The Sale of Goods Act does apply to second-hand goods. When considering whether goods are of satisfactory quality one must take into account the obviously lower expectations of things that have already been used. For example, you couldn't expect a ten-year-old bicycle to be without a single dent or with its paint as good as new. Second-hand goods will have worn parts which obviously can't be expected to last as long as those on a new model.

Sale goods

For these you have full rights under the Sale of Goods Act but if they were reduced because of a fault that was brought to your attention at the time or if you examine the goods and see an obvious defect, you would not be able to get your money back later.

One-day sales

Typically these are sales in which the sellers are not local. They will hire a venue such as a church hall or hotel or take a short-term lease on an empty shop in order to sell anything from electrical goods to carpets, for example. When you buy goods from a sale like this you are entitled to the usual safeguards: that the goods should be of satisfactory quality, fit for their purpose and as described. However, it will probably be virtually impossible for you to enforce your rights after you have bought from a dodgy one-day sale like this as the seller will have packed up and disappeared and will be practically impossible to trace.

THE TRADES DESCRIPTIONS ACT

This Act makes it an offence if a trader applies a false trade description to any goods or makes certain kinds of false statements about the provision of any services, accommodation or facilities. Remember that if something offered sounds too good to be true, it usually is.

A false description is not just a minor inaccuracy, it has to be obviously applied to the goods in question or their containers or labels. Local Trading Standards authorities are obliged to enforce the provisions of this Act and can seize the goods if necessary. It is not their job to get you compensation but they can investigate and take steps to prevent others being fooled. In the last resort it is up to you to enforce your legal rights by taking the trader to court in a civil action. No one else can do that for you. Before considering that, however, get advice from your Citizens Advice Bureau or Consumer Advisory Service.

What is a trade description?

A trade description is an indication as to the quality, size or gauge of goods (e.g. 'this bedspread is 70 cm × 90 cm), how they were made or processed (e.g. 'hand-sewn'); what they are made of (e.g. 'solid brass'). It can include their fitness for purpose, strength, performance, behaviour or accuracy (e.g. 'waterproof'), or any other physical characteristics which they possess (e.g. 'fitted with disc brakes'). It can be a statement that the goods have been tested or approved by any person (e.g. 'these stockings have been approved by a medical doctor'); where they were made (e.g. 'Made in England'); when they were made (e.g. 'eighteenth century chest of drawers'); who made them (e.g. 'genuine Hepplewhite chair') or any other information about their history (e.g. 'Government surplus stock').

Doorstep selling regulations

If you buy anything at your front door you have the right to a seven-day cooling-off period (which the salesmen will not be anxious to point out to you), during which you may cancel an agreement to buy goods or services worth more than £35 from a trader who simply turns up on your doorstep without being invited or if his visit follows an unsolicited phone or doorstep approach. However, if, as the result of a leaflet, you phone them to ask for a free quote, you may be cancelling out the right to this cooling-off period. In the USA, if you buy something for more than $25 sold door-to-door, you have a three-day cooling-off period during which you have a complete right to return the product for a full and immediate refund.

The salesperson must tell you about your cancellation rights at the sale and must give you two copies of a cancellation form (one to send back and one to keep) and a copy of your contract or receipt. The contract or receipt should be dated, show the name and address of the seller and explain your right to cancel. It should be in the same language as the sales presentation.

Traders who fail to inform you in writing of your right to a cooling-off period are committing a crime. Door-to-door sellers must provide a notice setting out cancellation rights when any agreement is made. Failure to do so makes the agreement unenforceable. This is the case whether a deposit is paid or not. If you want to cancel an agreement made like this, you must write a letter to the trader and your letter will take effect from the time that you post it.

If you bought something such as a fitted kitchen and it is installed during the seven-day cooling-off period, you may cancel the contract but you could still be liable for the costs of delivery and fitting. These regulations apply to most doorstep sales but they do not apply to transactions involving land, mortgages, insurance, consumer credit and most other financial services.

Insight

If someone sells you a few tea towels and a handy clothes brush at the door, you are not going to be ruined if they turn out to be rubbish. But if someone rings your door bell and offers you cheap double glazing or solar heating in the roof and wants you to sign immediately, get rid of them at once.

Counterfeit goods regulations

It is against the law to apply a registered trade mark to goods or to make an exact copy of anything that has a registered trade mark without the permission of the trade mark owner. But fake or counterfeit goods, also known as 'pirated' goods, are widely available. Modern technologies mean that criminals can make sophisticated copies of well-known brands. The most common fakes include designer-labelled clothes, watches, perfume and cosmetics, alcohol, cigarettes, CDs and DVDs, computer games, vehicle parts and DIY tools. Of course, you may still be able to use your statutory rights as the goods may not be 'as described', but it's not always easy to track down someone who has sold you something fake.

What's wrong with fakes?

There are several reasons why you should not buy fakes. The goods may be dangerous – for example, cosmetics can sometimes cause skin rashes and fake car parts may cause accidents. Many fake goods are thought to fund drug dealers and people involved in organized crime. If you buy fake goods and they don't live up to your expectations you won't get any after-sales service or guarantees. Fake goods are essentially stealing from the copyright owner.

Making a complaint

Make sure you have a valid complaint before you set out on this often frustrating action. You will need the correct name and address of the trader; copies of all relevant documents; receipts, guarantees, reports and any relevant letters; your reference number, agreement or account number.

COMPLAINING BY PHONE

Make a note of what you want to say; have receipts and other documents handy; get the name of the person you speak to; note the date, time and what was said; follow up your call with a letter.

COMPLAINING BY LETTER

Keep the information brief and to the point; use bullet points; describe the item you bought, say when and where you bought it and the cost; describe what was wrong with it, what you have done so far and the result; say what you want done to remedy the situation (e.g. if you want a refund or a repair); keep copies of any letters you send; send copies of previous letters you have sent or received – keep the originals.

> NOTE: If you've raised a serious complaint that you feel has not been dealt with satisfactorily, ask to speak to the company's highest authority, the Managing Director or Chief Executive. Some retailers are given a target as to the maximum acceptable number of chief executive complaints their store can be associated with. Sometimes this is motivation enough for the issue to be resolved quickly.

In the USA

In the USA there is no all-covering Sale of Goods Act.
Nevertheless, whether you buy through catalogues, over the
phone, online, door-to-door or on the internet, as a consumer you
have rights in these situations and businesses selling products have
responsibilities they must meet. There is legislation on specific
purchases such as motor vehicles, property and even jewellery.
Your rights may vary from state to state. The Federal Trade
Commission in the USA has a website providing information on
personal finances, major purchases and investment, consumer rights
and identity theft (www.ftc.gov). It has leaflets on many aspects of
consumer protection and a website covering home purchase and
home repairs, car purchase, doorstep selling and much more.

General information from US government-funded sources includes
the following sensible points:

- *Don't buy on impulse or under pressure.*
- *Ask family, friends and others you trust for advice based on
  their experience. Gather information about the seller and the
  item or service you are purchasing.*
- *Review product test results and other information from
  consumer experts.*
- *Check out a company's complaint record with your local
  consumer affairs office and the Better Business Bureau.*
- *Get a written copy of guarantees and warranties.*
- *Get the seller's refund, return and cancellation policies.*
- *Ask who to contact if you have a question or problem.*
- *Know who you are dealing with – don't do business with
  any company that won't provide its name, street address and
  phone number.*
- *Protect your personal information – share credit card
  information only when you are buying from a company
  you know and trust.*

- ▶ *Take your time: resist any urge to 'act now', despite the offer and terms. Once you turn over your money you may never get it back.*
- ▶ *Read the small print. Get all promises in writing and review all documents carefully before paying any money or signing a contract.*
- ▶ *Decide in advance exactly what you want and what you can afford.*

10 THRIFTY CONSUMER TIPS

1 *Think before you buy. It's much thriftier and more satisfactory than sorting out the problem later.*

2 *Learn by heart the three salient points in the Sale of Goods Act: that products should be 'of satisfactory quality', 'fit for purpose' and 'as described'.*

3 *If you are dissatisfied with a purchase, take it up with the shopkeeper in the first place. If he will do nothing, it may be worth writing to the manufacturer (although generally speaking he is under no legal obligation to you).*

4 *If you need help, talk to your local Citizens Advice Bureau or other objective advice organization, or if your local authority has a consumer advisory service, talk to them.*

5 *Before considering legal action, read about the Legal Advice Scheme and about Legal Aid.*

6 *Keep all documents, letters, agreements and notes about telephone calls in a safe and easily accessible file.*

7 *Remember that if you have been coerced or wheedled into signing a contract for goods to a doorstep seller, you have seven days (or three days in the USA) in which you can cancel the agreement, no matter what the seller tells you.*

8 *If you are sent something 'out of the blue' which you have not ordered then you can treat it as an unconditional gift – in other words you can keep it or give it away, sell it, use it or destroy it and the trader cannot expect you to have to pay for it. It is a criminal offence to demand payment or threaten legal action to obtain payment for unsolicited goods or services.*

9 *If you decide to complain about a product, do so as soon as you can, while you still have the memory of the transaction and, importantly, the papers and references.*

10 *When buying something valuable, make sure you read the contract carefully, read the small print and make sure you understand it, so that you know what you are letting yourself in for.*

QUICK REVISION TEST

1 What are the three things the Sale of Goods Act insists on when buying goods?

2 How long have you got to cancel an order if you have signed an agreement with a doorstep salesman?

3 If you want to make a claim under the Sale of Goods Act, who should the claim be made against?

4 If you want to make a complaint by phone, what should you have to hand before making the call?

5 Who should you go to for advice if things go wrong?

3

Thrifty money matters

In this chapter you will learn:
- *how to work out a budget*
- *about avoiding debt*
- *how to find investment advice.*

There are hundreds of organizations offering advice and special deals whether you are trying to get by on a shoestring, to save, or simply to get out of debt. Try to find unbiased advice. There are three types of adviser. An Independent Financial Adviser (IFA) will research the whole market on your behalf for a fee or on commission; a Tied Agent can only advise on the products of one provider; a Multi-Tied Agent is allowed to recommend the products of a limited selection of providers, rather than just one. DON'T be bullied into buying financial 'products' that you don't want; DON'T buy anything that you don't need.

Budgeting

Insight

If you don't use a computer to do your budgeting, buy yourself a simple hardback accounts book, available at any stationer. Such a book will last several years and give you the pleasure of keeping your accounts in a businesslike way.

If you keep track of money coming in and put aside what you need for bills and essential expenses like rent and food, you should have money left to save and some to spend. Try and save money each month for future projects or to cover emergencies. Be realistic. There's no point in deciding to cut down on the housekeeping if you can't bring yourself actually to buy less. On the other hand, try the challenge of managing on less. You can budget weekly, monthly or annually. Your budget might look something like this:

Income:

- *Wage, salary, freelance fees or occasional payments. If the amounts are different each month, average them over three or six months.*
- *Income from savings or investments.*
- *Any benefits you are paid.*
- *Maintenance from an ex-partner for you or your children.*
- *Contributions from other members of your family.*
- *Rent from any lodgers.*

Expenses:

- *Housekeeping including realistic amounts spent on food, toiletries, school dinners and meals at work, cleaning materials, cigarettes, sweets and pet food etc.*
- *Housing costs including mortgage or rent, second mortgage or secured loan, buildings and contents insurance, service charges and life or endowment insurance cover attached to your mortgage.*
- *Income tax.*
- *Local taxes.*
- *Fuel and water charges.*
- *Telephone charges.*
- *Travel expenses, including both public transport and the cost of running a car, such as road tax, insurance and maintenance.*
- *Childcare costs.*
- *TV licence and any TV rental costs.*
- *Clothes.*

- *Entertaining and meals out.*
- *Medical and dental expenses.*
- *Support for elderly relatives.*
- *Savings plans.*
- *Newspapers, books and magazines.*
- *Loan repayments.*
- *Money set aside for unexpected events.*

Saving

> **Insight**
>
> Interest rates vary, of course. In a recession they may dwindle to practically nothing. Look for ways in which your savings can bring in at least some interest (ISAs, for example).

Saving is probably the most useful thing you can do if you don't have much money but you want to make the most of it.

- *Decide how much you want to or are able to save regularly and bank it separately to your current account, where it will attract the most interest.*
- *Ask for any interest to be added to the account. You may be surprised how even a small amount, saved regularly, can quickly build up into a useful sum of money.*
- *Other ways to save are to buy into a short-term investment saving scheme. You may get a tax concession for joining such a scheme. The longer your money stays in the scheme, the better, but at a pinch you can draw out all the money if you need it.*

BANK DEALINGS

- *Packaged bank accounts cost a small amount a month and claim to offer perks and benefits in the form of such things as mobile phone insurance, an interest-free overdraft, a 24-hour legal helpline, travel insurance and so on. Most of these benefits you will already have through your service providers or your own insurance. It's usually better to buy products separately and negotiate the best deal individually.*

▶ *If you receive money regularly, paying bills by direct debit can save you money and is a convenient way of paying automatically. If your incomings are irregular or if you forget to monitor your accounts, be wary of direct debit which may pay out money which isn't in your bank account, thus creating an 'unauthorized overdraft'.*

▶ *Direct debit is probably the best way of paying the phone or broadband bill; there is often a surcharge for customers who do not pay this way. Most of the main gas and electricity suppliers offer discounts if you pay by direct debit.*

▶ *Be warned, car and household insurers may charge extra for people spreading their payments over the year.*

▶ *Question your bank charges. Many banks illegally charge customers for overdraft charges and automated letters. Telephone or write to your bank and get a refund.*

Thrifty thoughts about credit and debit cards

Credit is basically borrowing and at an expensive rate unless you pay it off on time. If you can't do without, get a cheaper credit card. Despite fees, there are still competitive 12-month interest-free balance transfer deals that are preferable to paying the lender's standard card rate. However, an interest-free credit deal has its pitfalls. If you don't repay the full amount before the end of the free interest period, you could find yourself paying the full interest, even if you are just one day late.

▶ *Ideally, if you must pay for goods by credit card, you should pay back the whole sum you owe each month and within the interest-free period. If you feel you can't pay back the whole amount monthly try to avoid only paying the minimum repayments.*

▶ *If you can't clear the balance every month consider a low-cost
   loan as an alternative: a credit card debt of £2,200 ($3,300)
   over three years will cost £545 ($820) in interest, whereas a
   loan at six per cent will cost £420 ($630): a saving of £125
   ($190). However, loans with variable interest rates can
   become more expensive than the card debt.*

▶ *The quickest way to get rid of credit card debt is to arrange
   the lowest interest deals possible. It is worth asking your
   current lenders if they would give you a lower rate – tell
   them you are thinking of changing cards and they might be
   persuaded. Haggling, contrary to popular opinion, is quite
   often effective in the money world.*

▶ *Stop buying anything on your credit cards (cut them up and
   throw them away). Pay the minimum amounts on the least
   expensive cards and as much on the most expensive card as
   you can manage until you've paid off that debt, then move
   on to the next most expensive. This may take years but it
   is possible and, of course, the more thriftily you live in the
   meanwhile, the quicker you will be able to do it.*

Borrowing money

The thrifty advice here is – DON'T. Of course most people do have
to borrow to buy a house, but otherwise make your borrowings
as small as you can. Most consumers are unaware of the real cost
of borrowing. To get an indication, ask your bank to calculate a
personal loan with a couple of missed payments or late payments.
And ask them to calculate the cost of paying out early. The
answers can be shocking but it is better to know than not to know.
If you must borrow, do it sensibly and make your borrowings as
small as you possibly can for the shortest possible period.

Insight

Some years ago I cut up all but one of my credit cards and
limited my use of the one I had left. It's amazing how much
difference this can make in the amount you spend/borrow.

Thrifty home ownership

The most expensive item you are ever likely to buy is your home. If you don't happen to have the ready cash, make sure your mortgage is the best available for you. There are thousands of deals to choose from so make sure you have some objective advice. There is plenty available on the internet but professional guidance is to be recommended.

▶ *Don't go directly to your bank or building society if you are looking for the cheapest mortgage deal. Although you may be used to dealing with them for other money matters, they may not reward your loyalty by offering the best deal on a mortgage and their range may be limited. Speak to at least one mortgage broker as they often have exclusive deals. A broker will also be able to advise on the type of mortgage that might suit you.*

▶ *Check that they will search the whole market for you as some brokers offer only a limited 'panel' of lenders. Also ask whether they charge a fee for their advice. All mortgage brokers receive commission from lenders when they arrange a mortgage but some also charge borrowers a fee on top of this and some are fees-free. Competition in the market is enormous.*

▶ *Don't pay the first fee an estate agent quotes. Haggle and play one off against another.*

▶ *Why not advertise your home yourself and eliminate the estate agent? You can do this through your local paper or through a specialist magazine or journal catering for the sort of person you think would appreciate your home.*

▶ *Get your solicitor to quote a fixed fee for conveyancing otherwise you may be shocked at the final fee.*

▶ *Grants or tax credits may be available for certain home improvements such as making your home more energy efficient by way of such things as improved insulation or a better boiler.*

▶ *Instead of using estate agents, think of a house swap. You pay little or no deposit and no stamp duty if you don't receive too* much top-up money to make the exchange equal. Get your home valued by several estate agents. Take an average price and put a photo and details in the local paper and newsagents' windows in the area you want to move to stating what sort of property you are looking for.

▶ If you want to move to a more expensive house a builder or developer may take your old home in part exchange.

▶ Sell large pieces of furniture before you move, especially if you are downsizing, to save on removal costs. You'll be glad not to be tripping over them when you move on.

Dealing with debt

It is a marvellous feeling, but very unusual these days, to be debt-free. Many people are well aware that they have a mortgage to cope with but forget that their credit card and other debts are piling up inexorably and so is the interest on them. Happy is the thrifty person who has plenty of interests, enough to live on, doesn't mind a frugal lifestyle and owes no money. But debt can creep up on the non-thrifty unawares. Getting into debt can start with just one small unpaid bill, but it soon mounts up. You may owe money on loans, overdrafts and numerous credit cards.

There are four immediate pieces of advice if you discover you are in debt.

1 *Don't panic. Even if you are heavily in debt there are a number of possibilities for sorting out the situation of which bankruptcy is a last resort.*

2 *Don't ignore the debt – it won't go away.*

3 *Don't invest if you have a debt. It is always better to use spare cash on repaying the debt rather than investing it.*

4 *Do go immediately to an objective advisor such as the free Citizens Advice Bureau (see your local telephone book) or the not-for-profit Debt Advice Trust (www.debtadvicetrust.org; call free on 0800 954 6518) or visit www.ftc.gov in the USA.*

Insight

Monitor your incomings and outgoings. Don't just glance at the lowest sum you have to pay back – look at what you actually owe. And don't get into debt at all if you can help it.

NOTE: Beware of debt consolidation companies which promise to help you to consolidate your bills into one monthly payment without borrowing and to stop credit harassment, repossessions and to wipe out your debts. Apart from not always receiving the best advice, you will probably be responsible for legal fees if they suggest you have to become bankrupt, as they often do. Get impartial, free debt advice from one of the many charitable or government-supported organizations.

Don't borrow any more money. You may end up paying a lot more than you borrowed with extremely high interest rates. It will help your advisors if you take certain practical steps as soon as possible. For example, collect up together all the information you can about your money affairs, then decide how to deal with the situation. An advice bureau can help you draw up your budget and help you write to your creditors. A sensible plan might look something like this:

1 *Make a list of all the people and companies to whom you owe money (your creditors). You will need the following information for each debt:*
   ▷ *the name and address of the creditor*
   ▷ *the account or reference number*
   ▷ *the amount you owe.*

Keep the latest letter or statement for each debt together in one folder so that you can easily find them if you need them. If you have received any court papers or letters that seem urgent, you may need to act quickly. If you are not sure from the papers what you should do next, get advice straight away from an experienced advisor such as the Citizens Advice Bureau (CAB).

2 *Decide which are the 'priority' debts – the ones you should deal with first.*

Priority debts include:

▶ *mortgage or rent arrears*
▶ *fuel arrears*
▶ *local tax arrears*
▶ *court fines*
▶ *arrears of maintenance payable to an ex-partner or children*
▶ *income tax or VAT arrears.*

Non-priority debts include:

▶ *benefits overpayments*
▶ *credit debts such as overdrafts, loans, hire purchase, credit card accounts and catalogues*
▶ *student loans*
▶ *money borrowed from friends or family.*

If you don't make any offers to pay, without explaining why, your creditors may take you to court.

3 *Work out your budget*

List all the income and expenses for your household. Be honest and make sure the amounts are realistic.

Add up the figures and you will see if you have any money left over to pay your debts. Perhaps you could even make some savings.

The Debt Advice Trust is a UK-registered not-for-profit organization, which helps people with impartial advice on getting out of debt. The Citizens Advice Bureau gives free advice on solving legal, money and other problems from 3,000 branches. The Consumer Credit Counselling Service (CCCS) is a registered charity, which helps people in financial difficulties by giving them free, independent advice. In the USA, the Debt Advice Bureau is a not-for-profit debt advisory service.

NEVER go to a debit management company before getting objective advice.

Never ignore letters from your priority creditors. Contact them as early as possible and let them know that you are having problems. Try to make an arrangement to pay back what you owe. Most organizations will be more helpful if you approach them first. If you phone, follow it up with a letter confirming what you said on the phone. Keep all correspondence. If you can't afford to pay anything to your priority debts and your situation is not likely to improve, the outcome may be very serious. Get advice straight away.

Sorting out your non-priority debts will depend on whether you have any money left from dealing with the priority debts. If you have money, you might be able to arrange a debt management plan but these often require a fairly high up-front fee. If you have no money left, you will probably have to ask your creditors to write off your debt or apply for bankruptcy. It is again best to follow the advice of a bureau such as the CAB or other objective organization.

Don't be afraid to bargain and haggle with your creditors. Don't accept no for an answer if you receive a letter rejecting your gesture offer of paying off £20,000 ($30,000) at £1 ($1.50) a month. Write back politely offering £1.50 ($2.25) and pointing out that if they don't accept you may have to go bankrupt in which case they will lose all possibility of getting any of their money back. Remember, as long as you owe them money they will not want to lose you. But do remember to get objective advice first.

Tax matters

TAX-FREE SAVINGS

Check whether you can save some money tax-free. In the UK you can save up to £5,100 a year in a tax-free savings account called an ISA. You don't pay tax on the interest accrued so if you have spare cash in your current account you could be earning up to £150 a year on it, instead of nothing at all.

BENEFITS AND TAX CREDITS

Check if you may be eligible for any benefits or tax credits. A tax credit is not a tax you pay, it is money that you receive regularly. Finding out if you are eligible may take some time and some dedication initially but you may find you are eligible for some worthwhile credits. Tax credits may be paid to you through your wages or straight into your bank or building society account. The sort of credits that might be available include:

- *Child Tax Credits, which may be receivable if you are responsible for a child or young person who normally lives with you.*
- *Working Tax Credit: if you are in work but on low pay this credit could top up your earnings, whether you are employed or self-employed. How much you might get will depend on whether you have children, how much you earn and other circumstances.*

WORKING FROM HOME

▶ *Tax deductions: if you are self-employed and working from home don't overlook invaluable tax deductions you can make for certain costs involved in using your home as your office. You can probably deduct a portion of your rent or mortgage interest and utilities as a business expense. You can also deduct a percentage of the telephone bill and various home maintenance expenses. It is worth checking with your tax advisor to make sure you are making the most of using your home as your office.*

▶ *Entertainment of clients: if your work involves necessary entertainment of clients or potential clients to discuss a current or future project, you may be able to deduct a portion of your entertainment costs. Ask your accountant's advice because such deductions are not always accepted.*

▶ *You can also deduct a percentage of mileage for use of your car for business. This figure usually changes each year so check with your accountant or your income tax office at the beginning of each year.*

▶ *Costs of travelling to meetings, interviews or other aspects of your business should be included.*

WHEN TO PAY BILLS

Insight
Whether you are organized enough to pay bills at the thriftiest times or not, do at least pay them before the due date or you will incur penalty payments.

▶ *If your utilities suppliers give discounts for early payment, pay early. If they don't it's to your advantage to pay your bills, including utilities, taxes and suppliers, as late as possible without incurring a fee. The longer you keep your money in the bank, the longer it is earning a return for you rather than for someone else.*

▶ *You will have to work out whether getting a special deal from the utilities by paying direct debit, as they will want you to do, is a better deal than paying when it suits you.*

Getting the most from insurance

Car insurance is mandatory. You have to have it by law if you drive. But do you really need all the other sorts of insurance brandished in front of you? Some forms of insurance are strongly advisable. For example, if you are a home owner, you would be glad of your insurance if your house burned down.

Travel insurance is also a good idea. For older people this can become horribly expensive but some airlines won't take you unless you have this insurance.

Life insurance only benefits those who come after you but may be mandatory if you have a mortgage.

Once you have eliminated unnecessary insurances, shop around for those you do want. You can go through a broker and find the cheapest/most satisfactory insurance without doing the work or you can do your own broking through the internet, which does take time but can produce cheap deals. You can compare hundreds of policies in one evening.

Many people do not realize that they automatically have life insurance from their employer. Check on this before buying your own policy.

Buildings and home insurance: don't necessarily buy yours from the bank or building society arranging your mortgage or home loan. You may get a better deal from some other insurance provider, so shop around before you decide.

You may be able to get slightly cheaper home insurance by fitting approved locks and alarms or by being a member of a local neighbourhood watch scheme.

Banks and other lenders may offer insurance policies to cover loan repayments. These may be useful but shop around for the best offer.

Finally, remember to pay your insurance premiums annually rather than monthly. If you pay monthly you are probably being charged a premium of between 15 to 20 per cent in interest.

CAR INSURANCE

▶ *You may save money on car insurance by switching providers every year. But try shopping around for cheaper quotes and getting your existing insurer to match them.*

▶ *Rather than pay to protect your no-claims bonus, save the money to pay for small claims yourself to avoid claiming on your insurance where possible.*

▶ *Look out for policies that reward environmentally friendly behaviour such as low mileage. There are discounts ranging from 5 to 15 per cent for running an eco-friendly engine.*

TRAVEL INSURANCE

▶ *Travel agents often cash in on selling insurance with the holiday. Single trip insurance can be what you need if you don't travel much in a year but shop around and don't necessarily buy it from your travel agent. If you go away more than twice a year including weekend breaks, you may be better off with an annual policy.*

▶ *Travel insurance that you get as part of a credit card package often only covers travel accidents while on a train, plane or hire car paid for on the card, so don't imagine this means you're covered for falling down the holiday villa stairs.*

▶ *Family travel insurance is cheaper than individual insurance. Insurance for the elderly is exorbitant and if you reach 80 it can become very difficult to find travel insurance at all. Try going through one of the organizations for the elderly such as Help the Aged.*

> **Insight**
>
> Britain's NHS has reciprocal health schemes in certain European countries so don't forget to apply for subsidized health treatments and take your card with you when you travel in these countries.

▶ *Don't be persuaded to upgrade to platinum cover with the offer of huge medical expenses you almost certainly won't need.*

▶ *Medical insurance may be a good thing if you might need treatment in a hurry, but if you have any faith at all in an existing national health service, do you really want to spend the money? It might be better to simply save that money to pay for private treatment directly, should you need it.*

▶ *If you do want to take out insurance, check that it is not already available free or at a reduced rate from your employer.*

▶ *Remember medical insurance does not cover accident and emergency treatment or palliative care. Most insurers will refuse to pay for drugs and treatments deemed too expensive by the NHS.*

▶ *Healthcare Cash-plan Scheme. If you are well organized, you could save money by taking out such a scheme. They are cheap to buy and allow holders to claim back money spent on dental and optical bills, plus a range of other healthcare costs such as physiotherapy. You may even be able to claim back 100 per cent on dental and optical bills but most people forget to claim.*

Thrifty investments

Investment is usually taken to mean the purchase of something such as valuable goods, stocks and shares or property in the expectation that it will increase in value and even provide an exceptional return. The thrifty will always take professional advice before making any investment and will beware of unsolicited or unexpected approaches offering investment opportunities of any kind. Always check on the credentials of any company, even if they appear gentlemanly and invite you to a day's seminar in a smart hotel with lunch thrown in.

Do not believe anyone who tells you that an investment will produce guaranteed, risk-free or exceptional returns. Never be pressured into making a quick decision and never sign up to anything immediately. A reputable dealer will always allow you time to think about an investment and do your own research – if the investment is genuine, there should be a cooling-off period in case you change your mind.

Ask about payment of commission. Do not accept an up-front commission payable at the time of purchase instead of the time of sale. Be very suspicious if you are told the deal is confidential. Why should it be?

Never give your bank account numbers, credit card numbers or other personal information to anyone you don't know or whose credentials you have not checked.

INVESTMENT SCAMS

Investment scams always appear more attractive than conventional investments with exaggerated claims for return on your money. As with so many money-related offers – if it looks too good to be true, it probably is.

Don't be seduced by an approach by phone or email to invest in high value goods such as champagne, jewellery, paintings or perhaps timeshare holiday apartments. A glossy (but misleading) brochure, fake quotes from 'leading newspapers' and graphs showing how well the goods have performed are not to be trusted. The goods are made to seem difficult to obtain without 'expert' assistance. Often they don't actually exist at all or have very little value or investment potential. The price paid will not appreciate or it will take years before the goods even reach the value at which they were bought.

Don't be seduced by pyramid schemes, chain letters or other types of scheme where a return depends on persuading others to join.

WHERE TO GET INVESTMENT ADVICE

> **Insight**
> Wherever you get advice, don't lose sight of your own common sense. And never be persuaded to put all your eggs in one basket. Then if one scheme goes down the drain, at least some money may be safe in another scheme.

- *Financial consultants: there are three kinds of these, independent financial advisers who must survey the whole marketplace to find the best product for your needs. Make sure their charges for fees or commission are clarified before you ask the advice. Tied agents are attached to one insurance company and paid commission by that company and don't normally charge a fee. Check the person is still connected with the life insurance company they claim to represent. Multi-tied agents can recommend a limited selections of providers.*
- *Solicitors: some solicitors can give financial advice but they must say so prominently on their writing paper and in their offices. They must give independent advice and most charge a fee.*
- *Accountants: many accountants are authorized to give financial advice and they must not be tied to a single financial services company.*
- *Stockbrokers: their main function is to buy and sell shares but many also give advice on all aspects of financial planning.*

10 THRIFTY MONEY TIPS

1 *Put as much money as you can into a tax-free savings account, such as an ISA.*

2 *Don't run up an overdraft without talking to your bank. You will be charged for unauthorized overdrafts.*

3 *Know the difference between secured and unsecured lending. If you take out a secured loan, you are using your house as surety and may lose it if you cannot make the loan repayments.*

4 *Don't wait until the last minute to file your Tax Return, especially if you think the taxman owes you money. The earlier you complete your return, the earlier you will receive a rebate and be able to get it to earn interest for you rather than it going to the Government.*

5 *If you are anxious about your money situation, tell your partner. Family help and support may help your solution as budgeting and saving will be a joint effort.*

6 *A mortgage company's insurance is not compulsory. Most people take the buildings insurance offered by their mortgage lender. But you don't have to. Your mortgage lender may charge you a small fee if you go elsewhere but you can still save money by shopping around.*

7 *If you swap insurers, keep the previous insurance policies. Your new insurers may refuse a claim for subsidence if they think it started while you were insured with a different company. If this happens, you will need to make a claim on your old policy.*

8 *If considering home improvements, such as a more efficient boiler or roof insulation, check whether you qualify for grants or tax credits.*

9 *Immediately delete emails without opening them, chain letters or other unsolicited approaches promoting get-rich-quick schemes.*

10 *Smoking and life insurance. Smokers pay on average 50 per cent more for life insurance so if you quit smoking, remember to apply for a new policy. How much you will actually benefit will depend on whether you've had any medical problems since taking out the insurance and how old you are.*

QUICK REVISION TEST

1   *What should you list under 'income' when working out your budget?*

2   *Write down all your expenses for one month and add up the cost.*

3   *What is a secured loan?*

4   *Who should you approach initially if you want to take out a mortgage?*

5   *Who should you approach as your first port of call for advice if you get into debt?*

6   *What can you include in your expenses if you wish to get tax deductions when working from home?*

4

Beat the bills

In this chapter you will learn:
- *about organizing your paperwork*
- *how to save on fuel bills*
- *about making the most of grants and benefits.*

Monitoring the paperwork

It's almost impossible to be successfully thrifty without being well-organized. Good money management means that bills and receipts need to be kept together and well ordered so you can find them when you need them and understand them when you find them. You don't need much room for this but you need to set aside a shelf with filing boxes and a nearby desktop or kitchen worktop to put them on. Even if you do your banking on the internet, there will be paperwork to deal with and if anything at all goes wrong, such as being late with important payments or misunderstandings with any of your suppliers, you should be able to lay your hands on the correspondence easily. An ordered filing system, however small, will make it much less daunting to check up on your bills each month.

There are numerous types of suitable storage available from businesslike box files to coloured A4 size stacking plastic or cardboard boxes, as well as concertina files to more serious little filing cabinets on castors that can be wheeled under a table or worktop when not in use.

Your 'money-management' centre is a useful place to keep all the important documents and records you own, such as your passport, insurance documents, bank statements, guarantees, handbooks, information on your credit cards, pension plans, investments, tax papers, deeds to your house and such things as birth and marriage certificates. Keep them in separate well-marked folders so that you can find anything you need at the drop of a hat. Cardboard folders are inexpensive in stationery shops and you might find them even cheaper in second-hand office equipment stores. When papers become out of date, throw them away to prevent confusion when searching out the current ones – but be careful not to throw the wrong papers away. If in doubt, keep everything for seven years.

Keep an address book, either in your mini office or on your computer (backed up). This should include:

▶ *bank and building society details such as contact numbers, addresses and account numbers*
▶ *similar details of all your insurance policies such as buildings, contents, life, medical, travel etc.*
▶ *similar details of any investment schemes you may have*
▶ *all your car papers*
▶ *all pension plans with names and contact numbers/addresses and personnel you may need to get in touch with*
▶ *contact details of any helplines – for reporting lost or stolen cards, for example*
▶ *contact details of any personal advisors such as accountants, stockbrokers or insurance brokers*
▶ *a copy of your will.*

Insight
DO make a will. If you don't your nearest and dearest will suffer. Whatever you leave will be undercut by lawyers' fees. Probate can last for years and in the end it is the rightful inheritors who will suffer.

Reducing your fuel bills

If you believe that efforts to diminish energy use in the home are practically meaningless, think again. Fossil fuels are not going to last forever and global warming is a warning against greedily using them up anyway. The rarer they become, the more expensive they will be. In fact, individual householders can do a great deal to reduce bills and this will make a difference not just today but to the following generations. Think of them too.

Thrift in fuel use doesn't need a tremendous effort or a great outlay in money. Quite small adjustments in the way homes are run can save meaningful amounts on bills. There are plenty of opportunities to be thrifty here. Governments are now taking the energy consumption of individual households very seriously and there are many schemes, grants and advice organizations to educate, advise and help in practical ways. The thrifty will avail themselves of these services as quickly as they can. With gas and electricity bills rising all the time it is important to find the best deal for each household.

If your suppliers give discounts for early payment, pay early. If they don't it's to your advantage to pay your bills, including utilities, taxes and suppliers as late as possible without incurring a fee. The longer you keep your money in the bank, the longer it is earning a return for you rather than for someone else. You will have to work out whether getting a special deal from the utilities by paying direct debit, as they will want you to do, is a better deal than paying when it suits you. If your income payments are irregular, you may not want to commit to direct debit which may try to pay out before your money has come in.

CHEAP AND CHEERFUL INSULATION

Make sure your home is efficiently insulated. Less fuel is used in insulated homes and less pollution of the environment occurs through the burning of gas, oil, coal and other fuels so fewer toxic fumes escape into the air. Although it is not possible to eliminate all loss of heat, you can reduce wastage considerably by insulating your home with thermal materials. Even if you adopt only the cheapest and easiest measures, you can still reduce the heating costs of your home by about half. You can keep warmer by generating a little heat and keeping it in than you can by generating a lot of heat and letting most of it escape. In many homes losses through the roof account for 15–30 per cent of all the heat that escapes. In a bungalow, which has a comparatively large roof space, the loss is even greater, whereas if you live in the middle storey of a residential block you will be largely insulated by your neighbours and so lose less. If you do have a loft, insulating it should pay for itself in about three years.

Obviously the most effective thing to do is insulate the whole house. Any gaps will allow heat to escape and ruin the effect. But some methods of insulation are much cheaper and easier to do than others and if you begin with those you will have made a good start.

Draught proofing

Insight

Draught proofing can be done by practically anybody and costs hardly anything. So do it. In the past I've used insulating tape for sealing up rattling windows during winter but now there are lots of cheap insulating strips you can get to keep out draughts.

The cheapest, quickest and most immediately rewarding way to prevent wasting heat is to prevent draughts. It is by far the cheapest form of insulation, giving the quickest return in energy conservation and saving on fuel bills. You can probably seal the whole home in one day and the materials are inexpensive and easily available.

Between 10 and 20 per cent of the heat loss of a whole house can be accounted for by draughts but this varies depending on the age and condition of your home. In an old house, where the woodwork has warped, cracks have appeared and general wear and tear has produced gaps and holes, draughts will be a major problem. The normal clearance between doors and windows and their frames is about 2.5 mm (⅛ in.). Taken altogether this could amount to a 1.2 sq m hole in your house, enough to make you very cold indeed on a bitter windy day. In many homes the situation is worse. Door and window frames may have warped and/or shrunk making the gaps much larger. So you can see why draught proofing should be taken seriously.

The worst problems are usually around doors and windows which no longer fit properly, through unused open fireplaces and joins between skirting boards and floors. Hold the back of your hand up to doors or windows and you will be startled at the strength of the cold and how the wind plays onto your fingers. Check the bath waste outlet; quite a chilly breeze can blow through there when the wind is in the wrong direction. Do not forget the ceiling hatch into the loft and the letter box in the front door, also keyholes and door latches.

Quick and easy draught proofing ideas
Windows:

▶ *Use insulating tape to seal windows. Various types are available from DIY and hardware stores. The cheapest are rolls of self-adhesive foam strip which you stick round the edges of the frame to fill the gaps. They stick to both metal and wood and are invisible when the doors or windows are closed. They don't last for ever and tend to get dirty quickly so you may have to replace them every two or three years. Prepare the surfaces by washing and wiping over with white spirit to make sure the strip will stick. Even thriftier is to use your child's plasticine or play dough to seal up the gaps.*
▶ *Keep some windows closed throughout the winter which will make sealing them much easier. As a temporary measure, stick masking tape across the gaps round window frames, unused doors and the loft hatch.*

Doors:

- *The bottom of the exterior front door is likely to be the cause of your worst draught problems. The cheapest and easiest draught excluder for doors is a plain strip of wood or plastic attached to the bottom of the door with an edge of bristles or rubber which brushes against the floor. More sturdy and complex excluders are available for ill-fitting or badly warped doors.*
- *Don't seal the tops of internal doors. Draughts are not worrying at this height and they bring in some necessary air.*
- *The old-fashioned device of hanging a heavy curtain across a front door to keep out draughts can be attractive as well as effective.*
- *A traditional draught excluder is the 'floor dog', usually in the shape of a snake, stuffed with old clothes, which nestles up to the door to keep out cold air. This can be inconvenient and might be an invitation to trip up for the elderly or the very young.*

Fireplaces:

- *Block up any fireplaces if you don't intend to use them. A considerable amount of heat is lost through thermal currents going up the chimney and cold draughts coming down.*

A piece of chipboard or plywood or even a piece of cardboard cut to the right size can be wedged into place.

Floors:

- *If you have suspended floors a surprising amount of cold air can come up between gaps between the floorboards and between the floor and skirting board. Carpets alone will not be enough to keep these draughts out.*
- *Make a papier maché filler from torn newspaper and hot water. Apply it to the gaps in the floorboards and when dried stain it to match the floorboards. Smooth it down as you go along or you will have a lot of sanding to do afterwards. If the gaps are wide you might even glue in slivers of wood which can be sanded down to the level of the floor.*

▷ Nail strips of quadrant moulding to the base of the skirting once the gaps have been sealed. Paint the moulding to match the skirting.

Other draught sources:

▷ The letter box can be a cold and draughty opening. Build a large, roomy box and fix it to the inside of the door to collect the letters and contain the draught.
▷ Cat flaps can be incredibly draughty conveniences. Try to find one that closes tightly and stays closed or provide your cat with a litter tray and persuade it to live indoors during the coldest weather. Tape up the flap in the meantime.

> NOTE: Remember that your home does need a certain amount of fresh air. In most homes this is not going to be a problem; more than enough usually percolates through air bricks and provided those are kept clear, you need not worry about stopping up draughts elsewhere.

More quick and thrifty insulation ideas

▷ Apart from draught proofing the most cost-effective way to insulate your home is to add insulation in the attic. Much of a home's heat is lost through the roof. There are various forms of roof insulation including fibre pellets blown into the loft space and blankets made of mineral fibres or sheep's wool unrolled and fixed to joists.
▷ If you live in a terraced house or a residential block you will already be insulated by the homes next to or above or below you. But any outside walls should be insulated if possible and so should unfinished basement walls. There are various frugal ways of insulating walls.
  ▷ You can reflect the heat from radiators back into the room with radiator panels which have a layer of aluminium.
  ▷ Hang a large rug or heavy curtain along a big area of blank wall to create an immediately warming effect. Velvet is a good material for this and if it is lined, so much the better. Large patchwork quilts can turn your home into an insulated cell.

> ▷ Books can have an insulating effect if they cover the
> whole wall – like a library. Since paper is a bad conductor
> of heat, the warmth does not escape through the books.
> ▷ Wood insulates well and can be used in the form of
> matchboarding (tongue and groove panelling). The
> boards are fixed to battens on the wall and can be sealed
> or painted.
> ▷ Thick wallpaper, backed fabrics, cork, flock wallpapers,
> hessian and felt are all helpful insulators.

▶ Insulating your water tank is cheap and insulation jackets are
easy to install. On a previously uninsulated tank the energy
savings should pay for the insulation in a few months. Insulate
the pipes as well, while you are about it.

Don't waste your water

Insight

Water meters will almost certainly become compulsory in a
few years. That is when we will see exactly how much water
we use from day to day. Get a water meter installed now if
you want to monitor your own water use.

Most people take their tap water for granted. But imagine how
much water it takes for a family of five each to have a bath every
day, for the washing machine and dishwasher to be used once
or twice a day, to flush the lavatory using a full cistern dozens of
times a day, to water the garden and lawn with a sprinkler running
for hours every day, not to mention a hose used for cleaning the
car or the dog and for filling the swimming pool. No wonder water
is becoming scarce and therefore, of course, expensive.

▶ *Install a water meter. If you have a big home with few*
occupants you could halve your annual water bill by installing
a water meter. But check with neighbours who have already
become metered to make sure it will actually be cheaper.
Where water meters are not compulsory, don't get a water

meter installed voluntarily until you have discovered how much other metered people are being charged.

▶ *About 15 per cent of an average home energy bill goes to heating water. To save hot water take showers instead of baths (NOTE: A power shower uses almost as much water as a bath).*

▶ *Wash only full loads when using a washing machine or dishwasher.*

▶ *Install low-flow shower heads to reduce your use of hot water.*

Monitor your electricity

Professional advisors often advise clients to shop around for the cheapest gas, electricity and telephone deals. But remember that all the utilities companies are in competition and what is cheaper one year will probably not remain so for long. The changeover is often fraught with errors and in the confusion you may end up paying an extra bill. If you can afford the time and hassle, give it a go, but if your time is precious and you are not saving that much – don't waste time chasing rainbows.

How much are you wasting?

It's reckoned that eight per cent of electricity consumed at home is from items that are not being used, so don't leave the TV and other appliances on standby when not in use – switch them off completely.

▶ *Leaving unnecessary items on standby is said to cost each household in the UK alone an average of £37 a year.*

▶ *A traditional TV consumes 100 watts of power when switched on and about two watts on standby. Newer LCD and plasma screens consume up to 400 watts when on and about four watts on standby.*

- *You should be able to switch off most DVD players/recorders, hard disk records or video recorders bought in recent years without having to re-tune them as the machines usually retain their settings. However, some satellite TV receivers are best left on standby when not in use so they can receive updates.*
- *Chargers in the UK for devices such as mobile phones, computer peripherals and MP3 players are said to use enough energy to power 115,000 homes. They don't consume a huge amount of energy individually but those left plugged in waste millions of pounds and are responsible for a million tonnes of carbon dioxide every year. If a charger feels warm when it is plugged in without being attached to a device it is still converting energy.*
- *Turning the thermostat down by just 1°C can cut more than ten per cent from the average central heating bill.*
- *High-efficiency condensing boilers can save one-third on heating bills.*
- *Water heating can account for 14–25 per cent of the energy consumed in your home. You can reduce your monthly water heating bills by choosing the appropriate water heater for your home or pool and by using some energy-efficient water heating strategies. Traditional water heaters require a tank in which the hot water is stored.*
- *Instant or 'demand' heaters heat the water as you run it, meaning that you don't need a storage tank. They provide hot water at 7.6 to 15.2 litres (2–5 gallons) per minute. Gas-fired demand water heaters produce higher flow rates than electric ones. If your model cannot supply enough hot water to have a shower and run the dishwasher at the same time you can install two or more demand heaters.*
- *Look out for new 'smart meters'. Existing electricity meters only measure gross gas and electricity consumption but a new generation of 'smart meters' has a range of extra functions: for example, they can be read by remote control – so there will be no need for estimated bills; they display energy consumption in monetary terms rather than kilowatt hours, making them easier to understand; and they may include internet meters, allowing you to monitor where the energy is being consumed*

in your home and where it is being wasted (for example devices left on standby).

THRIFTY LIGHTING

Insight

Turn out the lights: hall lights, bathroom lights, bedside lights, desk lamps all get left on as though they didn't use energy at all. One light bulb might not break the bank, but leave two or three on permanently and you soon notice the difference.

▶ *Energy-saving bulbs use up two-thirds less energy and last up to ten times longer. If all households replaced just one light bulb with an energy efficient one, the money saved could pay thousands of family fuel bills a year, according to the Energy Saving Trust.*

▶ *Dimmers, timers and motion detectors on indoor and outdoor lighting all help to reduce electricity consumption. Or try offering your children five pence (ten cents) for every time they switch off a light in a room that nobody is using.*

▶ *If you are going out of a room for half an hour or even ten minutes, turn the lights off.*

▶ *Replace your five most-used light bulbs with energy-saving bulbs.*

GENERAL ELECTRICITY SAVING TIPS

▶ *During lunch hours and other 'dormant' periods, activate the 'sleep' features on computers and office equipment so they power down when not in use.*

▶ *Appliances account for about 20 per cent of household energy use. Limit the amount you use your washing machine – do you really need clean jeans every day? Switch to cold water washing of laundry – detergents formulated for cold water get clothes just as clean.*

▶ *When you next renew any electrical appliance, check that you get the most energy-efficient one; look for the EU Energy*

Efficiency label, or in the USA, the Energy Star label found on many products from TVs, boilers, refrigerators and freezers to light bulbs.

▶ Lower the temperature on your wash programme. Washing clothes at 30°C as opposed to 40°C uses 40 per cent less energy and is generally as efficient.

▶ Turn your heating down at night and whenever you leave home for a day or more. Better still, install a programmable thermostat to adjust the temperature automatically. Up to half your energy bill goes to heating and cooling so this is a worthwhile expense.

▶ Put on an extra jumper rather than turning the thermostat up when it gets really cold. If you live in a cold climate and you can comfortably wear a T-shirt at home you're wasting money.

▶ Take advantage of the sun's warmth – open up blinds and curtains in winter to back up your heating system.

▶ Clean or replace air conditioning filters each month. Dirty filters block air flow through your heating and cooling systems, increasing energy consumption and shortening the equipment's life.

▶ For window unit air conditioning, buy a plug-in timer and set it to turn off about the time you leave for the day, and to turn back on half an hour before you get home. This will use less electricity than having the AC constantly running. The simplest timers are very cheap.

▶ Use fans instead of air conditioning when possible. Fans cost less to use.

▶ A glass front or glass screen will reduce heat loss from an open fireplace.

▶ An electric blanket is much less expensive than heating a bedroom.

▶ Only heat as much water in the kettle as you need at one time. Most kettles have a minimum level for safety reasons but it is often enough to make two cups.

▶ Have a look at your electricity meter so you can see how fast it is spinning. Check which appliances make it turn faster and use them less.

▶ *When buying a new TV and recording equipment look for appliances that have two 'off' buttons, one on the remote and another that actually turns the appliance off.*

Cut your home phone bills

....
Insight

Is your land line phone absolutely necessary? Look at the bill –
perhaps your mobile and emails can take its place.
....

▶ *There are dozens of cheap phone companies from cable companies that package your telephone, television and even broadband internet access to low-cost dial-up services that give you access to cheaper calls using your existing line.*

▶ *Limit your time on the phone – land or mobile. If possible use fax, text or email instead. Skype is an internet method of speaking for the cost of emailing. Sometimes it makes the voice echo and sound peculiar but the technology is improving.*

▶ *Is your mobile phone really necessary? And if it is, do you use it more than you need or should? Why not leave it at home on days when you don't need it?*

▶ *Consider a pay-as-you-go mobile. If you pay £50 ($75) a month to your mobile phone company – that's £600 ($900) a year. People who use their mobile phone for emergencies or only for specific occasions can top up occasionally with as little as £5 ($7.50) which can pay for the odd call when you need it and can last for months.*

▶ *If you plan to make and receive many calls while abroad, buy a local pay-as-you-go SIM card. This will change the phone's number so you will need to let the relevant people know. Or contact your local network at least three days before you go away and ask for an overseas add-on package.*

▶ *Remember, you may have to pay to receive as well as send texts while you are abroad.*

Don't lose out on grants and benefits

> **Insight**
>
> It's easy to dismiss the idea of local government grants but, although applying can be a nuisance, it's often worthwhile so make the effort. At least find out if you are eligible for insulation grants or a more efficient boiler.

Check to see if you qualify for any government assistance with your heating bills, especially if you have a low income or are a senior citizen on a fixed income. There are various government and local government schemes to help you save gas and electricity and even help you pay for what you use. The Energy Saving Trust (EST) in the UK is a non-profit organization with local energy efficiency advice centres which encourages the use of cleaner, sustainable energy and energy efficiency and grants to encourage more efficient use of energy in homes and vehicles. Its website has free and impartial advice (www.energysavingtrust.org.uk). In the USA the Alliance to Save Energy (www.ase.org) and the US Department of Energy (www.energy.gov) both provide energy-efficiency information and tips.

▶ *You may be able to get a grant for insulation or to upgrade your heating system.*

▶ *The EST has a Priority Consumer Team who will help older people to switch suppliers or find deals suited to their needs and can advise on energy grants and free services they may be missing out on.*

▶ *If you are over 60, check with the Department of Work and Pensions to see whether you are eligible for a Cold Weather Payment in winter.*

▶ *In the USA, check which areas have the lowest gas or oil prices and heat your home with the energy that is cheapest in your area.*

▶ *Don't forget the sun. Consider installing solar panels. Even if you don't expect to stay in your home long enough to make back the money, it will increase its value. There are often grants for this kind of improvement nowadays.*

- *Check tax breaks and homeowner's insurance policies for savings when you add energy conserving items to your home.*
- *Check with your local electric company to find out if they have times during the day when the rates are lower.*

10 THRIFTY BILL TIPS

1 *In winter put on extra layers of warm clothing and keep the heating turned down.*

2 *Check how much cold wind is blowing in through your letter box and fix a sealed box with a lid to the back of the door to prevent the draughts.*

3 *Frighten yourself by sitting for a while and watching your electricity meter gallop round. Check which appliances make it turn fastest and turn them off or use them less.*

4 *Stop using your mobile phone to tell your partner you're on the bus and will be home in five minutes. Better still, leave it at home if you don't need it.*

5 *Dress your hot water tank in an insulated jacket. Jackets are inexpensive, available in sizes to fit standard tanks and only need to be tied on.*

6 *Look into the possibility of using new technology such as a small wind turbine or solar panels on the roof or in the garden to contribute to your energy supply. Improvements to their design and efficiency are happening all the time and you might even get a grant.*

7 *Check up from time to time that you have the best landline phone and broadband deal. There is a lot of competition and if you have time and energy to go through the actual process of changing, you could make worthwhile savings.*

8 *Consider being slightly less clean. Wash your jeans and T-shirts every two days instead of every day – you'll not only save on electricity for running the washing machine but you'll save on hot water too.*

9 *Look for the energy efficiency label when you buy a new appliance and look at the instructions to make sure it will do what you want it to in the most energy-efficient way.*

10 *Make sure you are receiving all the grants and benefits you may be eligible for.*

QUICK REVISION TEST

1 What's the first thing to do when undertaking to lower you bills?

2 What's the cheapest and most effective way to save on gas and electricity?

3 In what way are energy-saving light bulbs better than conventional ones?

4 What sort of shower head should you install if you want to save water?

5 Specify five ways in which you can insulate walls on the inside.

5

Internet know-how

In this chapter you will learn:
- *about buying a computer*
- *how to get the best from the internet*
- *about shopping online.*

Computer and internet know-how

There is no doubt that some people need a computer for their work and others wouldn't dream of doing without a computer in the home. If you run a business from home, are a writer, designer, student or simply have a busy life to organize, you probably own a computer anyway. Having your own internet account gives you freedom to access the internet at any time rather than having to rely on public terminals. Using the internet can be a way of saving a lot of money and time for those who actually have the time and the inclination to become familiar with it. You can access the World Wide Web and send and receive emails without owning a computer quite cheaply if you use an internet café, and for free if you go to your local library.

For some people owning a computer is an expense not worth the hassle. If you are elderly, don't see very well, find a keyboard difficult to operate and have no previous experience, then a computer might simply be too frustrating and confusing to be helpful. If you live on a pension or benefits, in a very small space, it might be better to use a library computer when you need to. If you want to get onto the internet and send and receive emails, you will need a landline telephone, and all the accessories that go with printing out messages. Why not save the money and use someone else's computer? At least in the beginning this will give you a low-cost and simple way to find out if the internet is for you. It is also a simple and cheap way to use the internet on an ongoing basis.

If you decide to do without a computer of your own, you can still send or receive email from any computer with a web browser and internet access. Computers can be found in various places including your public library, business centres in major hotels, airports, mainline stations, conference centres or internet cafés. Courses on using the internet are available in libraries and in local colleges.

Buying a computer

> **Insight**
>
> Modern laptops can be as simple or sophisticated as you want and prices are coming down. Do get advice from a knowledgeable friend so you are not paying more than you need for a computer that does more than you want.

So you do need a computer? In fact, most people do. Using a computer is essential for most children as a lifetime skill and as a tool for learning. From then on it will become more and more essential. Students require one and professionals find that many work contracts insist on email contact.

Buying a computer need not be inordinately expensive but you do need to research what's around and what's right for you. Apple computers are the ones used by most designers and architects or anyone who does much drawing. PCs are often preferred by people who mostly want to use the keyboard. Desk computers have larger screens and often larger keyboards which are comfortable when using the machine a lot. Laptops are often more expensive because they can be as powerful as large computers and, of course, can be carried around and even used on trains.

Computers are updating and evolving all the time. Last month's computer is already out of date. New technologies and improvements keep the price and complexity of a new computer high. The computer you need depends on what you want to do with it. If you want a computer for access to the internet and word processing you almost certainly don't need most of the newest technology. If you want to buy a new computer, buy last year's model if you can get one. If you are not comfortable with the technology, buy it as a package from a reliable retailer or make sure you get technical advice and help with setting up. It is usually best to buy your computer, printer and accessories by the same manufacturer so that they are sure to be compatible.

When buying your computer and accessories be sure to consider the following points as well:

▶ *If you are inexperienced, buy a complete package from a reputable department store. Look for packages which include the computer itself, your choice of monitor and accessories with everything you need to set it up plus a good selection of software and an after-sales service. For the more experienced there are many outlets where you can put together your own choice of equipment and get it all at excellent prices. Also check the clearance and end-of-line sections in the online sites of well-known manufacturers.*

▶ *An all-in-one scanner/copier/printer must be one of the bargains of the century. Unfortunately, the toner cartridges are not cheap. It's worth trying out some of the compatible alternative recycled toner and inkjet cartridges which are available from several sources. However, be warned, sometimes they don't seem to last as long and sometimes they are rejected by the printer. If this happens, don't waste any more money or time – go back to the correct ones. Three you might try are www.lasertech.co.uk; www.inkcycle.co.uk; www.atlanticinkjet.com.*

▶ *Reject extended warranties. Your computer should be under manufacturer's warranty, for the first year anyway. If something goes wrong after that it will probably be cheaper to hire someone to come and repair it.*

▶ *Laptops may be seductive but you could save hundreds of pounds or dollars if you are prepared to buy a basic desktop model. Larger computers are also much less likely to be stolen.*

▶ *Shop around for software at online clearing houses for discounted products from many manufacturers.*

Students:

▶ *If you are a student there may be discounts or rebates on computer equipment through your university or college. Some manufacturers offer student discounts directly through a participating college or university. You may be able to save around 15 per cent when buying a computer.*

BUYING A SECOND-HAND COMPUTER

Insight

For a child it may be better to have a second-hand computer than none at all. But for anyone using a computer for research, for communicating with others and for professional work, it's best for your computer to be no more than five or so years old.

Theoretically a second-hand computer should be as satisfactory as a new one. The trouble is, because technology is moving on so fast, computers more than five to ten years old may not be compatible with the newer ones that other people are buying. This might not matter if you just use it for your own personal benefit, but if you want to communicate with other people, and especially for work purposes, this could be a big handicap. However, there can be tremendous cost savings if you buy second-hand. You might get a discount of 80 or even 90 per cent on the original purchase price. Talk to friends or colleagues who have a bit of experience. Try the machine out before you buy it. Decide what printer, modem and other equipment as well as software features you will need and make sure they are compatible with the computer you have in mind. Make sure you have someone experienced at hand or at least some sort of support service in case you run into problems once you get the machine home. Don't pay anyone for sorting out a problem until they have actually completed the job.

DECIDING WHAT YOU WANT

Make sure you do some research about the various computer deals on the market. The Consumers' Association (a membership organization) in the UK or the US Consumer Information Center are good sources of information.

Support services tend to consist of:

▶ *Telephone help lines – This can be quick and easy but you may be charged for the calls and charges may be expensive so have all the relevant questions and information written down in front of you before you call.*
▶ *Online services – Many sellers now provide areas on their sites that list common problems and solutions and where you can ask for advice. Ask your seller how much it will cost to access such help. Sod's law says that if you have a fault on the computer, you might not be able to access the online repair service. Installation services may be offered by the supplier and might be useful if you haven't used a computer before. But again, there may be a charge for installation. A computer-wise friend, niece or nephew might help you for a free meal instead.*

Additional advice:

▶ *Don't be influenced by price alone. Look for quality so that the item will serve you well over a long time with low maintenance costs. A cheap item that breaks down is the opposite to a thrifty bargain.*
▶ *Look for standard, durable and competent technology that is as simple as possible.*

- *Look for equipment that is simple, easy to maintain and, if you need replacement parts or accessories, ensure that you will not have to buy them from just one particular company.*
- *Look for a neat, compact design that will be easy to absorb into the household.*
- *A laptop computer may look small but might cost a lot more. However, it can have at least as much if not more memory, fit into a fraction of the space and you can take it anywhere and use it on the train.*
- *A laptop costs less to run than a desktop computer. Energy savings can be tremendous especially if you run it from a battery at home as well as out and about.*
- *Check that your warranty will entitle you to technical support, repairs or replacement if your computer breaks down.*
- *If you want to upgrade make sure that the components are compatible. Take a list of your computer's specifications with you to compare with the products you wish to buy. New software may not be compatible with your system.*

THRIFTY RUNNING OF YOUR COMPUTER

Insight

Fit your computer use into your daily schedule. You might dedicate two hours in the morning and another two in the afternoon to computer work. That would free you up to spend other parts of the day on other activities and save on energy too.

A computer can use a lot of energy while running and add considerably to your electricity bill. So it is wise to have a strategy that encourages you to use the computer as economically as possible.

- *Although there is a small surge of energy when a computer starts up, this small amount of energy is still less than the energy used when a computer is left idling for long periods of time.*
- *Turn off the monitor if you are going to stop using your computer for more than 20 minutes.*

- ▶ *Turn off both the CPU (central processing unit) and the monitor if you are not going to use you computer for more than two hours.*
- ▶ *Ideally, you should unplug all the computer equipment when it's not in use to prevent it from drawing power even when shut off. However, most of us are human and can't be bothered to get down on hands and knees to locate the various switches, so buy a power strip/surge protector and make sure your monitors, printers and other accessories are operated by it as a group. When the equipment is not in use for extended periods, turn off the switch on the power strip.*
- ▶ *Discipline yourself to plan your use of the computer throughout the day; allocate specific hours to its use and turn it off at other times. The less time a computer is left on, the longer it will last.*
- ▶ *Use the sleep mode feature when breaking off work for a short time rather than switching the computer off completely and having to boot it up again. Sleep mode powers down the computer so that it consumes 15 watts or less power which is around 70 per cent less electricity than leaving it on.*
- ▶ *Screen savers are not energy savers. In fact, using a screen saver may use more energy than not using one and the power-down feature may not work if you have a screen saver activated. Modern LCD colour monitors do not need screen savers at all.*
- ▶ *Computer printers are among the big energy wasters. Some of them may use up to 11.5 watts even when idling. Keep your printer switched off except when it's actually running.*

ACCESSORIES

Inconveniently, accessories for computers change almost as quickly as computers themselves. The floppy disk had a relatively small capacity for information but then in came the shiny, much larger capacity CD-ROM. Now there is the memory stick, also known as flash drive or thumb drive, which plugs into the computer and has as much memory as your hard drive in a device the size of your thumb. It's an excellent way to store pictures and as emergency back up for important files on your computer or to transport

mountains of data from work to home and vice versa. It saves
a lot of money otherwise spent on CD-ROMs and it saves space –
in fact the main problem is that it's so tiny, it's easy to lose in a
drawer or pocket.

Computer uses

EMAIL

Many people use email as their main way of communicating rather
than using a landline telephone. It is cheap, quick and extremely
convenient, especially if you are working at your desk.

To get online you will first need to register with an internet service
provider. Take the advice of a friend or relative who is satisfied
with their provider. They will charge a small monthly fee, for
which you possibly get extra perks such as free pages for a website
and efficient help if something goes wrong.

There are many free email providers; again, seek the advice of
a friend. Once your email is established, find out how to delete,
categorize and file your messages. Like the clutter in your home,
clutter on your email gets in the way of efficient working. Even if
you delete messages, they are always recoverable.

KNOW YOUR VIRUSES, SPAMS AND SCAMS

The first thing to do before going online at all on your computer is
to install a virus protection programme. This is not an unnecessary
extra but an essential precaution. A good anti-virus programme
should protect you from more or less all the virus dangers,
provided you keep it up to date. If you use the internet a lot, get
one that includes firewall and other extra protection.

Spam is defined as unsolicited emails sent out in large numbers
and can be used to spread viruses. Spammers can get your email

address by buying lists from brokers that continuously harvest email addresses from newsgroups, chat rooms, websites, internet directories, and more. Spammers also run 'dictionary' attacks, throwing billions of combinations of words and numbers at an email database until it finds valid address combinations. If you receive an unusual email or an email from a sender you don't recognize, it could well be a spam – delete it immediately without opening it.

To reduce spam, don't display your email address in public, particularly not in newsgroups, chat rooms, websites, or online service directories. You should get to understand privacy policies and forms, and use opt-out options. Even scanning these suspicious emails in 'preview' mode can be dangerous. Delete them immediately, but most importantly, be sure you automatically update anti-spam, anti-virus, anti-spyware, and other critical security software to ward off attacks. Other popular spam-based internet scams include fake foreign lotteries, investment schemes, chain letters, credit repair offers, advance-fee loan deals, cheque overpayment cons, and work-at-home ploys.

Insight

Too much protection may mean you don't receive emails you would like to. There's a balance between good protection and overprotection so don't batten down the hatches against everybody trying to contact you.

HOAX EMAIL

If you use your email every day you probably get at least one hoax message a week forwarded by a gullible friend. Perhaps the most difficult to ignore are the chain letters concerning missing children. These might include sentences such as this: 'I am asking you all, begging you to please forward this email on to anyone and everyone you know. PLEASE. My 13-year-old girl has been missing for two weeks now...' This form of spam tears at the heartstrings and is difficult to ignore – in case it turns out to be true. But this is not the way to help the world. There is no way to update or recall a message once it gets onto the internet to millions of receivers.

Even if there ever was a child and that child was found, the email takes on a life of its own, spreading around the world for years. But it's more likely that the email was sent as a joke. Never forward email unless you know exactly who sent it to you. Comprehensive computer security software with a spam filter can protect you against much of this sort of hoax.

Email phishing is another sort of scam in which the email masquerades as a legitimate business communication from your bank, mortgage provider, credit card company, PayPal, eBay or other such organization. Spammers use these companies' domain names and set up fake websites. You may be directed to call a fake customer service phone number to give up your user ID and pin. A typical phishing scam might appear to come from Nigeria or Ghana informing you that: 'We are small scale Alluvial Gold dealers in the eastern part of Ghana. Now we have in stock about 1,500 kg of Alluvial Gold Dust. We can welcome you as middleman…'. Don't even take the time to read these through. Delete them immediately. They are not only scams they are dangerous scams and could get you into a lot of trouble.

Remember:

- *Never respond to email or pop-up messages that ask for your personal or financial information and don't click on links in the message.*
- *Anyone who emails you asking for your Social Security number or information about your bank or credit card account is a scam artist.*
- *Don't cut and paste a link from the message into your web browser: phishers can make links look as though they go to a genuine site but then take you to a lookalike site.*

RESEARCHING ONLINE

The World Wide Web has made researching any subject a quick, easy and exciting pastime. Finding information on the web is not difficult but you should be aware that much of it is unreliable.

It is not an edited, ordered or unified information package like a set of encyclopaedias. Anybody can put information on the web and many people get it wrong. Always look to see if the information is dated (sometimes it can be not months but several years out of date). Double check all information you are not sure about. Compare one website's information with another's and judge which is the most reliable before making use of it.

To research online follow these guidelines:

▶ *Non-commercial websites with objective advice and information (government or charitable, for example) are recognizable because they end with .gov or .org. This isn't foolproof because theoretically anyone can actually use these suffixes but it's an indication that the site can be taken seriously.*
▶ *If searching for reliable information, start with a large public library such as the British Library or the US Library of Congress.*
▶ *Trusted societies and organizations are useful for specialist interests such as the Royal Horticultural Society or the Royal Institute of British Architects.*
▶ *Look at several sites for information on a particular subject but use your judgement to decide whether they are reliable or not.*

MUSIC ONLINE

▶ *Save on an expensive stereo by downloading music onto a disc or iPod.*
▶ *Play your music through your computer. Today's computer speaker sets have clear high and mid-range sounds with clean bass. You should be more than satisfied using your computer as the stereo.*
▶ *If you have a music library set up in iTunes just buy a decent set of speakers and you'll have saved money.*
▶ *Most of the pay-per-song sites cost as much as if you bought a whole CD so save money by just buying your favourite singles.*

Shopping online

Insight

Remember that spur-of-the-moment purchases, however small, can build up very quickly so watch your eBay and Amazon purchases carefully and limit all internet purchases to a certain amount of money a month.

Websites have improved enormously in recent years; more goods and services are being offered online and the better ones are easy to negotiate so more people are making use of them. This sort of shopping-at-a-distance is undoubtedly convenient, usually efficient and often thrifty. It means you don't have to go traipsing around the shops until you find what you want. Online traders can sell more cheaply because there is no shop to run or maintain. However, goods sometimes take a long time to arrive because the trader wants to wait until there are enough orders to ensure a big discount from the manufacturers. What happens if the goods don't turn up? Or if you don't like them or they don't fit when they arrive? In the UK you have rights, similar to the Sale of Goods Act (see pp. 15–16) under the Distance Selling Regulations. They do not apply to financial services, or sale of land, although the thrifty would not be considering making such purchases online anyway.

You can protect yourself to some extent by dealing only with traders based in your own country. Goods from abroad can add huge unexpected delivery and tax charges. Some sites don't answer messages and they are not bound by the same consumer laws. Some internet traders don't list their phone number so you can't call them in case of a problem.

▶ *eBay is not necessarily the cheapest online shopping site. Compare with others before going for it, other sites may offer a better deal.*
▶ *Bid early in the morning and avoid auctions ending at popular times such as Sunday evenings.*

- *Don't give your credit or debit card details until you have ascertained that the company has a secure site by looking for the closed padlock sign at the bottom of the screen and look for information about the protection the company has put in place.*
- *The trader must give their name and a geographical address, not just a PO Box number and not just their email address, and must give an accurate description of the goods or services. Orders must be confirmed in writing.*
- *Shop around for the best deals and prices.*
- *The cooling-off period: the Distance Selling Regulations give you the right to change your mind and cancel an order within seven working days of receiving the goods. Check what the company's policy is on returning goods and find out who pays for the return postage. If they came from abroad, you may be faced with an expensive postage bill to return them. If you do decide to cancel, you should put this in writing either by letter (proof of postage certificate or recorded delivery would be wise) or fax or email. A telephone call is not good enough, unless both you and the trader agree otherwise. If you return the goods within these time limits you are entitled to expect your money to be refunded within 30 days.*
- *Watch out for high postage rates and other hidden costs such as VAT and other duty payable, particularly if goods are being sent from abroad. Goods sent from abroad may take some time to be delivered. Check with the trader how long this will take and set a delivery date that you must have them by. Where no delivery date has been agreed, delivery must be within 30 days.*
- *Try to get personal recommendations for companies you have not done business with before. Or get help and advice from specialist organizations such as Consumer Direct, a telephone and online consumer service operated by the Office of Fair Trading (a non-ministerial government department) or visit their website www.consumerdirect.gov.uk.*
- *Be wary of buying very expensive items from outside your own country unless you know the company well.*
- *Always print out or save the order (where you will be able to find it again) and keep any terms and conditions that appear on the website just in case of any disputes or problems later on.*

INTERNET AUCTION SITES

This is a popular way of selling. Many people who advertise goods on this type of site are private sellers. Your rights against a private seller are considerably reduced and are the same as if you answered an ad in your local paper. But the goods do have to be 'as described' as specified in the Sale of Goods Act. On an internet site it may be difficult to find out who you are dealing with. Some auction websites offer to resolve complaints but not all do, so read the terms and conditions carefully. If the person advertising on the internet auction website is a trader, you will retain your consumer rights.

Some safety checks:

▶ *Check the seller's reputation. Look at any feedback posted by previous buyers.*
▶ *Ask questions before placing a bid. Is postage included? Do you need extra insurance? Where does the seller live?*
▶ *In addition to the internet auction website's terms and conditions, the seller may have his/her own conditions. Read these carefully.*
▶ *Pay by credit card if possible. If the item is more than £100 ($150) you may have added protection.*
▶ *If somebody uses your credit card fraudulently or dishonestly (without your knowledge) for any kind of distance purchase, you can cancel the payment and the card issuer must refund you. You should notify your card issuer as soon as possible after you discover this fraudulent use.*
▶ *Buy from a legitimate site. It's easy to get taken in these days in online transactions unless you are familiar with the websites. Just about anyone can set up a domain name and start offering goods. So, how can you protect yourself? There are several online sites that can help if you are unsure, among them:*

whois.net which lists the person or company that registered
the site and when it was registered. If the site is very new you
should be suspicious. If you don't know the site by name or
reputation, always check it out before you buy.

....

Insight

If your credit card is used dishonestly without your
knowledge DO cancel the payment and notify the card issuer
AS SOON AS POSSIBLE after you discover the transaction.

....

REBATES THROUGH SHOPPING PORTALS

When internet shopping, find what you want not through
specific retailers' web pages but through a shopping portal. This
is a separate free website that has an arrangement with certain
retailers who pay a commission in return for the portal linking
them to clients like you. If you buy something, the retailer pays
the portal a commission and the portal shares that commission
with you – so you get a rebate and a good price. Choose a portal
that has commission affiliations with retailers you are likely to
shop at. A typical rebate is about five per cent. Two to try are
www.fatwallet.com and www.hotdeals.com.

Shop bots or shopping robots are special websites for finding the
cheapest prices of particular products. They can seek out dozens
of prices on the web in 30 seconds. Most people click into a well-
known retailer such as Amazon to find what they want but if you
go to a shop bot and search it will compare prices from lots of
retailers. You then click on the one you like to get to the retail site.
Two major shop bots which vet the retailers are www.kelkoo.com
and www.pricerunner.co.uk. Some sites focus on specific categories
(such as DVDs or books) and are often less commercially driven so
they may have a wider choice.

BUYING FROM ABROAD

The internet has made it much easier to buy from overseas but
make sure you are aware of the potential problems. Standards
and systems vary between countries. Ask the supplier to confirm

the compatibility of goods, e.g. electrical goods. Check if any guarantee is valid in your country. You may have to return the product to the supplier's country if there is a problem. Check for hidden costs such as VAT, customs duties, delivery charges, postage and packing. If problems arise you might have to take legal action in the country of the seller.

10 THRIFTY ONLINE TIPS

1 *If you are new to computing, see if your local library runs free courses for beginners.*

2 *If you know someone who changes their computers frequently to keep up to date with the latest technology, get them to pass on an old computer to you. Even if you have to buy a new printer to go with it, you will have saved a lot of money.*

3 *Don't miss out on any special deals and packages available through your work or, if you are a student, through your university or college.*

4 *If you are debating whether to buy a desktop or laptop computer, remember that although laptops cost less to run they can be stolen more easily, often cost more to buy and usually cost more to repair.*

5 *Turn your computer to sleep mode when leaving it for 20 minutes or more and turn it off completely at night or when leaving it for the day.*

6 *Don't allow your printer to sit idling. It uses a lot of power even when not in use.*

7 *When buying a new monitor, choose an LCD model which doesn't need a screen saver because screen savers use a lot of power.*

8 *Save shelf space and money by storing information on a memory stick (otherwise known as a flash drive or thumb drive) instead of onto CDs.*

9 *Don't make a false economy by not installing virus protection software. A bad virus can cripple your computer. AVG Free and avast! Free are both reputable free anti-virus programmes.*

10 *Before buying from a website, check that there is a phone number or other form of contact address in case of problems.*

QUICK REVISION TEST

1 *If you are buying a new computer, should you go for the latest model?*

2 *Why use the sleep mode on a computer?*

3 *What should you do if you receive an email from a source you don't recognize?*

4 *What are the website address suffixes that indicate a non-commercial website which is liable to have objective information?*

5 *Why is it best to pay for online purchases with a credit card?*

6

The fine art of haggling

In this chapter you will learn:
- *how to haggle*
- *about haggling on home soil*
- *about haggling in markets.*

Haggling is a form of negotiation that takes place in many parts of the world when one person has something to sell and another wishes to buy. People in the Western world, where large branch stores and supermarkets price up their products on a universal basis, often find the idea of bargaining for products embarrassing or demeaning. But where individuals are selling products they have made or collected for sale themselves and where time is not of the essence, haggling is a centuries-old and accepted form of trading and one that is both interesting and satisfying, since the wished for outcome is that both parties should feel they have come out of the contract satisfactorily. There is nothing to stop anyone from haggling, particularly in outdoor markets both at home and abroad. Only your Western reserve may inhibit you so fight it and take the plunge. In fact the inveterate haggler won't be put off haggling in unlikely situations/places and you may be surprised what you can get away with, even at home if you're prepared to give it a go. But remember, the point of haggling is not simply to get the best deal for yourself but to come to a mutually beneficial agreement in which both you and the seller feel satisfied.

How does haggling work?

Haggling is the process in which the vendor offers goods at a particular price and the buyer offers a lower price. Gradually the offers and counter offers work their way towards a mutually satisfactory price somewhere in the middle. Basically it's a process of negotiation. In countries where haggling is the accepted method of coming to an agreement on price, it is foolish to buy in any other way. In fact it is really an art form in its own right. As with any other type of negotiation, there is a protocol to haggling but the basic skill is to have some inside knowledge about the value of what you are buying and setting a limit to what you are prepared to pay.

The process can be expected to take some time and often there is a good deal of play-acting involved. If you are negotiating for something valuable, the seller may hospitably offer cups of tea or coffee and snacks, perhaps even a chair to sit on. You can accept these with a good grace, but they don't mean you have to buy anything. Haggling is not so much a question of getting the cheapest price or getting the better of the other person, but of working one's way towards an appropriate price so that each party feels they have come out of the transaction well.

In general, both buyer and seller have a notion of what the correct price should be so it's a question of working towards that price. Intelligent haggling can add to the spice of buying objects when on holiday and in certain situations in one's own country too. Becoming a skilled haggler can spice up the process of buying things no end.

Haggling is most effective if you are buying valuable items such as gold, jewellery, carpets or furniture where the difference between the originally mentioned price and the finally agreed sum can be quite substantial. If you want to obtain a bargain, be prepared to invest some time and have a rough idea what the item is actually worth. If you are buying more than one item, a discount can be expected for buying in bulk so you might consider getting a group of three or four people together to contribute to a 'lot'.

It is worth pointing out any defect in the goods you want such as the fading colour on a cotton fabric, a missing button or a poor finish on a shirt. This should entitle you to ask for a discount on the asking price.

Insight

Bargaining is an accepted form of reaching a mutually acceptable price for buyer and seller in many parts of the world. It should ideally be good natured, leisurely, unfraught and finally satisfying.

How to haggle:

1 *Choose a haggle-friendly environment.*
2 *Choose an item and decide on the maximum price you are prepared to pay.*
3 *Start by offering a much lower price than the seller originally suggests. The seller will bring his price down in small increments and you should offer a slightly higher price each time until very gradually a price is reached that is acceptable to you both.*
4 *Never go over your maximum price.*

Try to have a rough understanding of the object's reasonable market value before you start haggling. You can get an idea by looking at government run craft shops and hotel gift shops which generally have fixed prices that will at least give you an upper limit. Don't offer a price straight away. Market sellers and small shops expect a bit of haggling and will set their prices higher than what they actually hope to receive. Let the seller tell you the price he's asking and negotiate from there. The initial price may seem ridiculously high but that's just part of the game. So don't necessarily be put off but respond with a ridiculously low price. Throughout your bargaining don't forget to stick to your original maximum price and never go above it. In fact, have three prices in your head before you start: the most you are prepared to pay;

an average price which will be acceptable; a rock bottom price which you don't really expect to achieve. If you can't get the goods even at your top price, just walk away.

Good haggling is a lot to do with play-acting and a lot to do with bluffing as in poker. This should be understood by both parties. Act surprised when the sales person tells you the price, then just keep quiet and let them try to justify the price. More often than not they will add a few extras or bring the price down without you even having to ask. Keep your sense of humour and remain polite and friendly. You are much more likely to get a good price if you are not abusive. If the seller takes a liking to you, you are much more likely to get a better deal in the long run.

Insight

If you want to haggle over a fault in an item, do it straight away – don't wait for several weeks when you are much less likely to convince the retailer that the fault was theirs not yours.

If you are going to try and get an item cheaper than its offer price, do so with an air of confidence. Don't sidle up hesitantly, as though embarrassed, but march up briskly as though you expect your offer to be accepted. This is much more likely to succeed than an apologetic mumble. Bargaining in the right situation is always worth a try but do it with style. Do not feel you have to complete the transaction immediately, particularly if you are bargaining for a rug or an antique or something expensive.

Before you make an approach take the trouble to learn a little about the merchandise you are looking at. Make a list of the points you want to look for or ask about. Don't belittle the merchandise. Most marketers are proud of what they have and much of it is handmade, interesting and different – after all that's why you want it. Quite often if you make some sort of human contact with the seller you may get a more reasonable price simply because he's flattered by your attention. By taking an intelligent interest in his wares you will be much more likely to get his goodwill.

Universal haggling strategies

▶ *Shop on days and at hours when trade is slow.*
▶ *In vegetable and flower markets shop late in the day when vendors are anxious to get rid of perishable merchandise.*
▶ *Don't lose your temper; being polite and keeping your cool is much more effective.*
▶ *Be patient.*
▶ *Start to walk away as though losing interest – that often encourages the vendor to drop the price.*
▶ *Establish a rapport with the vendor; in foreign markets, learn a few words of the language; go back to examine the merchandise for a few days in succession; see if the price comes down.*
▶ *Indicate you've had a similar object offered for less at another stall.*
▶ *Offer to buy three or four objects at a discount (if you want them, of course).*
▶ *Point out any flaws in the product – that might get you a discount.*
▶ *If you can't come to an agreement, try holding out the money you are prepared to pay. The sight of cash in hand may be enough to sway the vendor.*
▶ *Bring your money in small denominations. Trying to get change for the equivalent of a £20 ($30) note when items are selling for 99p ($1.50) can be difficult, expensive and gives the message to everyone that you are rich.*
▶ *Always be willing to leave empty-handed if the price is not right.*

Haggling on home soil

Large, high street, chain stores where things have a clearly labelled price and the sales force can't make price decisions are not good places to start haggling. You won't have much luck trying to haggle in supermarkets, grocery stores, bus depots or major retailers, where the pricing is not in the hands of the sales personnel (although occasionally it does no harm to ask, especially if an object has some flaw.) Nor is it usually worth bargaining in discount stores where the prices are already reduced. However, the skilled haggler may be able to get bargains through negotiating in certain types of store or market-place, such as craft and food markets; bazaars and street markets; second-hand and junk shops; jumble, garage or car boot sales; antique shops and Oriental carpet stores.

Insight

Take your time when negotiating a purchase. Don't be pressured into making quick decisions and make sure you really weigh up the pros and cons of the situation.

▶ *Private sales of anything present good haggling opportunities because the seller usually wants to get rid of the item quickly.*

▶ *It's nearly always worth haggling if you are buying a second-hand car. You can't expect to get a car at half price but you could probably negotiate for new tyres or a ten per cent reduction in price.*

▶ *Electrical, electronics, carpet or furniture stores are the most likely to offer deals and independent stores are a better bet than chains. The more you buy, the more likely you are to get a better deal with free delivery and installation at the very least. For example, you may be able to get a computer package with added accessories or free warranty by negotiating with the sales person, especially if they are on commission. In Singapore in the huge electronics and camera stores, you would be considered pathetically naive if you didn't expect to get an extra carrying case or a couple of spare batteries when buying an expensive item. In smaller shops you may find the proprietor willing to give you discount for a cash sale.*

▶ *You can haggle productively for certain services such as getting building or gardening work done, perhaps for catering, dressmaking and other individually offered services.*

▶ You can often haggle over the cost of a stay in a hotel, guest house or B&B even if there are set prices. For example, you might get a worthwhile discount if you are prepared to stay out of season or during the week rather than at weekends. If you are staying for a longish period (more than two weeks, say) or you are reviewing the hotel for a large number of tourists who will be following on later, be sure to let the hotel know this. If negotiating over hotel rooms it may be easier to haggle over the telephone or by email – and in good time before your stay.

SOME HAGGLING TACTICS IN YOUR HOME COUNTRY

▶ Visit any store at a quiet time rather than a busy Saturday afternoon when the weekend staff are not only harassed but probably don't know much about the products. If the sales person says they don't have the authority to negotiate, ask to see the manager.
▶ When buying something expensive, like a car or a computer, arrive at a mutually satisfactory deal, then say you have to get the approval of a partner. This may bring the price down again slightly or bring an added extra so as not to lose the sale.
▶ Gauge whether the seller is more interested in selling for a high price or negotiating a quick sale – if the quick sale is important, quickly offer a lower price.
▶ Often if a seller sees cash-in-hand he will accept what you actually have in your hand, whereas if you want to pay by cheque or card, he will stick out for a higher price.
▶ Appear shocked at the initial 'outrageous' price quoted.
▶ During negotiations remain silent for a while and wait for the seller's patience to wear out first.
▶ Don't get angry or make a scene. Some people feel that will tip the situation in their favour but in fact in a market it will embarrass the whole area and in a store the staff will probably call security and turf you out as quickly as possible.
▶ Don't expect to get away with an unreasonably low price.

- *Even shop prices are simply an 'invitation to tender'. You are free to make a lower offer for anything, and the shop assistant is free to laugh in your face at the suggestion – but if the object has a flaw you may be lucky.*
- *Try haggling when renting a car. You may be able to negotiate a free day or unlimited miles, for example.*

Insight

Over the age of 75? Many car rental companies won't allow you to rent. This example of ageism unfortunately exists in many countries. If you've tried all local companies without success, try getting your own car insurance transferred to the rental car.

- *Sales staff often get a bonus if they sell warranties to go with goods they sell. You may be able to bargain to get the product itself at a cheaper price if you buy the warranty as well. You then have the right to cancel the warranty within 14 days, with a full refund of the insurance money.*
- *Student discounts are not necessarily limited to NUS card holders. If you are in further or higher education part-time or at an institution that doesn't provide you with a NUS card, try negotiating with the retailer who may be willing to accept another form of student ID.*

COMPENSATORY PAYMENTS FOR BAD SERVICE

Sometimes you may be able to bargain with service providers or others who have given you a bad deal to give you something to compensate for the inconvenience and hassle.

If you have switched service providers, for example, and the original provider keeps billing you, why not ask for a goodwill payment to make up for it? Don't ask for compensation, ask for a goodwill payment. That makes them feel better and more likely to accept your suggestion. Make it a written request, be extremely polite and make the suggestion of how much money you want e.g. £50 ($75) for a botched switch from one service provider to another, £10 ($15) for each direct debit that wasn't paid for any reason. It's always worth asking and you might be pleasantly surprised by the response. Make sure whatever you ask for is reasonable. Just because somebody made a foolish slip up and inconvenienced you doesn't mean you are entitled to a fortune.

Always remember, if you complain, do so in the nicest possible way and by letter. Phone calls can slip away into the ozone but letters have to be answered and may be seen by other people. If you get no satisfactory reply when complaining, write to the Managing Director or Chief Executive. Something often gets done very swiftly if you do that.

Haggling in foreign markets

Haggling is the tradition, and indeed has become an art form, in nearly all foreign markets, including China, South-East Asia, Turkey, Arabia, Egypt, Africa and South America, where it is perfectly legal to haggle, bargain and ask for a discount. Look for local produce and handmade merchandise. On holiday much of your shopping may well take place in places where the seller has laid out his or her pottery or hand-woven wares by the side of a famous temple or waterfall as well as in the markets and bazaars and small, individually owned shops. Although haggling is the norm for shopping in markets and souks you should not try to haggle in small supermarkets where the stock is computerized or in fruit and vegetable markets where the prices are so small anyway that they are not worth discounting.

▶ *Set aside at least a day and wander round and see what catches your eye. Carry your purse and money in a safe place. Markets are seething with people, the perfect situation for pickpockets. The thrifty should know better than to get their pockets picked.*
▶ *In many countries, genuine antique items cannot be exported without permission and some things are illegal anyway, such*

as ivory. In any case, why not buy something that a living local artisan has so carefully and skilfully produced?

▶ *Once you start seriously negotiating you will be expected to make the purchase if you reach a reasonable agreement. Never be affected by somebody getting irritated or shouting. It is all too easy to be brow-beaten and bullied into buying something far too expensive and in no way a bargain.*

▶ *Make sure you can convert the currency you are bargaining with into your own. Take a calculator or currency converter. Then when somebody offers you a price you don't have to do any currency conversion, just reply with a lower price.*

And remember, nobody is in a hurry except, possibly, you. Take your time. Enjoy it but don't waste your time or the seller's time by bargaining if you have no intention of buying.

▶ *For your own convenience make a decision about what is not worth haggling for. Items below the equivalent of the price of a sandwich, for example, are hardly worth the effort of wasting your precious holiday time so don't waste it haggling over trivia. Agree a price and hand over the money with a good grace. Your bargain of the year will probably end up collecting dust behind the bookcase or in the local charity shop anyway.*

▶ *When buying expensive items make up your mind what you do actually want and then haggle for all you're worth, but be prepared to pay a little over the odds for something really worthwhile, particularly if it is handmade and representative of the country you are visiting.*

▶ *Don't feel sorry for the vendor. Nobody's going to sell you anything out of the goodness of their hearts. This is how they make their living. Sob stories such as 'My child will not eat now' or 'My wife needs medicine' (even if true) are all part of the play-acting.*

▶ *Never let the seller know how much money you have or are willing to spend and try not to let them see how interested you are. If you have researched the object and know what level of price makes sense, the vendor will be more willing to take you seriously.*

- Consider offering other items apart from money as payments. Western T-shirts, earrings or baseball caps might be taken in exchange for an embroidered silk bag or a carved elephant.
- Take your time, and drink your cup of tea if you are offered one. You are not rushing to the office and the seller has all day.
- Avoid obvious tourist traps such as railway stations and airports where prices are always hiked up.
- Don't buy things you can buy just as cheaply at home.
- Remember you are going to have to take the items home. Will they go on the plane or will you have to ship (and insure) them?
- Ask about tax refunds. Many countries will refund the value-added tax, usually on purchases over a certain amount, when you leave.

Insight

Remember that individual merchants in foreign street markets are almost certainly much less well off than you are. Scoring off them by getting a ridiculously cheap price for something you like is nothing to boast about.

Once you've started negotiations, it may be hard to get away so make sure you really are interested in the object first. If you are buying something cheap, haggling is more of a form of human contact and done for form's sake. But if you are buying something expensive such as gold, try to take a local friend with you or ask your tour guide to give you an idea of the true value of an item. Traders can tell a rich foreigner a mile off and will put up their asking price accordingly. Shopkeepers will try to persuade you that they offer you the best value but will not be offended when you say you want to look around and would come back. Nearly always, you stand a better chance of getting a bargain late at night rather than earlier in the day.

In South-East Asia, retailers often speak limited English so your play-acting must come into force with a vengeance. Try to shop in the local currency as you will get a worse exchange for pounds or dollars than you would get at a bank.

Plan to buy items that the country or city is known for, for example:

▶ *Wines in Burgundy.*
▶ *Leather goods in Florence.*
▶ *Carpets, spices, and pottery in Arabia and north Africa.*
▶ *Tin artefacts, woven textiles and quaint ornaments made out of painted coconuts and beads in Mexico.*
▶ *Woven textiles in South America generally.*
▶ *Woven tapestries in Peru.*
▶ *In the Middle East you will find gold souks where you are supposed to be able to get gold at the lowest prices in the world. When buying gold, haggle about price per gram not the price per item. For other valuables you can always say a friend bought a similar item for less. Always negotiate with the manager and not some assistant.*
▶ *Arabian and North African markets offer every spice under the sun not to mention hand-woven carpets. In antique markets you can find coffee pots, Arabian chests, daggers, and carvings at excellent prices.*
▶ *Eastern Europe is one of the best places to pick up antiques because the countries were closed for so long and have only relatively recently opened up to trade, all sort of articles are appearing out of attics and basements and are now selling on the open market. In markets you can pick up everything from Communist relics to clothes, Russian dolls and other souvenirs. Find out what's made locally to get the best deals. For example, you can get lace and amber in both Estonia and Lithuania, but lace is made in Estonia and you'll get the best prices there. In Estonia you'll get a better deal on amber, which is the speciality of the country.*

10 HANDY HAGGLING TIPS

1 Practise haggling for small, unimportant items first. Haggling is a skill like any other and you can't expect to be the world's greatest haggler at the first try.

2 Make sure you know the object's reasonable market value before you start your negotiations or you could end up paying more than it is actually worth.

3 If you can't get the price below the maximum you allowed yourself – walk away from the deal. There are other shops and other stalls and other versions of the same object.

4 Don't put on all your best finery to go bazaar and flea-market shopping. Stall holders will set their prices higher the richer they think you are. At the same time, don't imagine they will think you are a pauper, whatever you wear. Tourists are, by definition, well-off people.

5 Don't be too particular over a couple of pesos. Tourists often take bargaining too seriously. Remember that the prices may sound a lot but once you convert them to pounds or dollars they are probably very reasonable and the few pesos or whatever you are haggling over may mean a lot to the seller.

6 Even in cultures where haggling is the normal way of buying, certain items do have fixed prices. Don't, for example, try to haggle for bus tickets, train tickets, bottled water, alcohol or groceries in a shop.

7 Don't let the other person 'lose face'. Be aware that the people you are dealing with are real people with real lives and responsibilities. Finding an agreed solution is the aim, not getting the better of someone else.

8 *It usually pays to learn a few simple words or phrases of the local language. For example: 'Hello'; 'How are you?'; 'How much?'; 'Too much'; and 'Thank you' are all useful.*

9 *Keep your sense of proportion and your sense of humour. Know when to accept an offer.*

10 *Shut up from time to time. There may be a silent battle as to who comes up first with another offer but the longer you can stay quiet, the more likely the seller will be to jump into the breach.*

QUICK REVISION TEST

1 *What type of product can you haggle for most effectively?*

2 *Is it worth haggling for special deals when booking hotel rooms?*

3 *How can you haggle for electronic equipment?*

4 *Name five haggling strategies you can use in street markets.*

5 *What should you NOT try haggling for – even abroad?*

7

Thrifty shopping

In this chapter you will learn:
- *how to get the best from large stores*
- *where to find cheap or discounted objects*
- *how to buy at an auction.*

Shopping in the twenty-first century is not just a necessity, it is a national hobby. It can be a family outing for the day, a way of spending a rainy morning over a pile of catalogues, or a way of making the most of internet opportunities. It can be an addiction. What's important for you as a thrifty person is to make sure that the purchases are of things you actually need and that you have actually bought the best of its kind for the most reasonable price. A shoddy object is unlikely to be a bargain, no matter how little you spent on it, since it probably won't work properly, may be unsafe and you will have to replace it long before you should have to. Seek out specialist shops if you want to buy specialist equipment (for example, outdoor equipment for camping, climbing or pot-holing) where you can discuss your needs with a knowledgeable assistant.

> ### Insight
> Stick to one credit card and one debit card for all your shopping and use them sparingly. Most individual store cards are an expensive waste of money not to mention a lure and a temptation.

Don't forget that you are entering into a legal contract with the seller and may be entitled to a full refund of the price you paid if you bought damaged goods. The thrifty shopper will know these rights and bear them in mind. Beware of special offers, price cuts and bargains. It's easy to be taken in by a 'ten per cent off' deal for yet another pack of candles you don't need or a 'three-for-two' deal in a bookshop when you've read all or some of the books on offer.

Online shopping is definitely a way to find good prices but there are plenty of 'physical' outlets and ruses for shopping cheaply as well and concepts like shopping villages are fighting back in terms of price and are also able to offer physical extras such as children's play areas and places to eat. This chapter looks at economical places to shop and gives guidelines on how to get the best and not the worst of shopping in the flesh.

Shopping in large stores

Beware of store cards. Many of these charge over 20 per cent interest which is incredibly wasteful, far more than a standard card. If you have been persuaded to get one, cut it up and throw it away. They are often offered at the till when you are buying a garment. It's difficult to resist the offer of 'ten per cent off your first buy with the store card'. Young people are particularly targeted, who love the ability to buy without appearing to spend and then rack up ill-affordable debts. One ruse is to accept a store card when making an important purchase, benefit from the discount for first use then go home and cut up the card. Many stores organize special store card holder evenings and offers, a bit like a membership club. There's nothing wrong with keeping a store card just for this – but don't carry it about in your purse – wait until you need it.

Make the most of any store with the promise of 'never knowingly undersold' in other words a guarantee that if you find the same product cheaper elsewhere the store will match the lower price.

This policy does not usually apply to online sales, because price comparisons are too complicated.

Large stores, particularly in clothes departments, are mainly season-led. The sales are often held at the end of a season to make room for the new season's stock. Don't buy for the present season. Unless you are a complete fashion prisoner, buy in the sales and keep the clothes until the weather is suited for them again.

Shopping know-how

▶ *If a supermarket over-charges you for an item, don't tell the cashier about the error. Take your goods and receipt immediately to customer services; sometimes they may refund the entire amount and even let you keep the goods.*

▶ *Companies need to keep your loyalty. If you are not content with a sale, politely complain. If your complaint is justified ask for compensation such as gift vouchers; the shop will probably agree in order to keep your custom. But if you complain and accept the shop's apology, the shop will assume that you are happy with the outcome.*

▶ *If you buy something at a shop and when you arrive home you find they have given you the wrong item, ask for travel expenses for getting back to the store. If you needed the article urgently that day you could even try asking for compensation (usually gift vouchers) for your time.*

▶ *If you break something in a shop where there is a notice saying 'all breakages must be paid for', you may not have to pay if you can prove that the shelves were poorly stacked or the item was sticking out or if there were other circumstances whereby it was not your negligence that caused the breakage.*

▶ *If you don't want to be encumbered with masses of packaging to dispose of, you are legally entitled to hand extra packaging (such as boxes or bags) back to the shop when you've bought something.*

Shopping in the sales

This can be a thrifty way of shopping but only if you use it well. First of all you must be sure not to be tempted into buying things you don't need simply because they've been reduced. Why buy a pair of shoes you will never wear simply because they cost £50 ($75) instead of their original £100 ($150)? All you have done is spent £50 ($75) which could have gone into the piggy bank. Here are some things you should bear in mind when venturing to the sales:

▶ *'Special purchase' often means that the goods have been bought in just for the sales and so may not be of the usual standard.*
▶ *Bargain items should always quote the higher previous price and you should not be left to guess what the reduction might be.*
▶ *If the shop uses a general notice saying 'half-price sale' the discount must apply to at least ten per cent of the range of products on offer when the sale begins.*
▶ *If you buy something in a sale you still have all your normal rights. Stores may say they don't give refunds. But if what you've bought is faulty they are obliged to give you a monetary refund or at least pay for the goods to be repaired.*
▶ *Don't be drawn in by a 'closing down sale'. Shops can have as many closing down sales as they like without ever actually closing down.*
▶ *Good buys in sales are likely to be school clothes after the first day of term, holiday wear in September, beach bags in August, Christmas toys and other gifts in January and Easter eggs the week after Easter.*

Insight

Are you temperamentally suited to shopping in large department store sales? If crowds upset you and you feel under pressure are you likely to make a bad purchase? Don't shop in the sales simply because they are there. Only do so if there's something specific you know you want.

Car boot sales and garage sales

Car boot sales are popular in Britain and in France and provide a venue in which private individuals can gather to sell their unwanted items. They nearly always take place at weekends, often in the grounds of schools and other community buildings or in fields or car parks. Sellers pay a nominal fee for their pitch and arrive with their goods in the boot of their car. Usually the items are unpacked onto folding trestle tables, a blanket or tarpaulin or simply on the ground. Entry to the general public may be free or there may be a small charge. Items on sale may range from old books, records, videos, toys, stamps, coins, radios, ornaments, tools, clocks, furniture, garden plants, paper, pens and stationery. Almost everything is sold at knock-down prices and much of the merchandise is likely to be worthless and much-used. It is easy to be seduced by the amount of 'stuff' into buying a lot of the kind of items that your cellar or loft is already full of.

Useful tips:

▶ *Go armed with a list of things you are actually looking for and enjoy looking at the paraphernalia but as far as buying goes, don't be tempted by anything not on your list.*
▶ *To find car boot sales look in local papers, or keep your eye open as you drive through the countryside on a Saturday.*
▶ *Advertised opening times are often not strictly adhered to and in many cases the nature of the venue itself makes it possible to get in a bit early for a good look at what's on sale.*

NOTE: Second-hand items may not conform to up-to-date safety guidelines, especially when being sold by private individuals who may themselves not be aware of these regulations. The thrifty will avoid electrical goods such as irons or electric fires; nightwear, foam mattresses and furniture, which may not meet modern flammability requirements; toys with sharp edges or points or small parts that can be pulled off and may be a choking hazard. It's also unwise to buy prams, baby buggies, paraffin heaters or oil heaters.

Discount stores

Small discount shops have a medley of household goods consisting of anything from Christmas lights and DIY tools to toys, felt pens, batteries and handbags. You can often find ordinary household products and objects and many may be perfectly safe and most are very cheap indeed. But your thrifty side should be immediately suspicious of things that are so cheaply priced. Where are the safety labels? How long is an item likely to last? If it carries a well-known manufacturer's name, is the name genuine? Recently a toothpaste bought in a US discount store was discovered to contain diethylene glycol, a chemical found in antifreeze. Although the toothpaste was labelled as 'Colgate', Colgate-Palmolive Co. said the imported tubes were falsely packaged counterfeits. CDs, DVDs, handbags and sunglasses are also often sold in discount stores under well-known names but which are actually fake. The owners of the discount stores themselves may be victims of these fakes, but whoever is responsible, be careful what you buy. Very cheap Christmas lights will probably not last any longer than one season and may be electrically unsafe as well – although if you find a good-looking travelling toiletry bag, you may really have hit on a bargain. When buying cheap leather goods, particularly bags and slippers, check the lining as paper is often used on imported products instead of leather.

Cash-and-carry shops

These are the shops that supply retail shops with goods. You can get anything from food and drink to garden equipment and hardware at wholesale prices. You will need to be introduced by a friend who is a caterer, retailer, or professional business user (someone who pays VAT), or be registered as self-employed or be able to show two invoices addressed to you from suppliers, or your name as a director on company-headed paper. You must also be prepared to buy in wholesale amounts so make sure you have somewhere to store ten bumper packs of toilet rolls or a freezer's worth of chicken livers.

> **Insight**
>
> Bulk buying can save money for certain goods, especially if you can share what you buy with friends and neighbours. But do your sums and make sure the prices really are cheaper in bulk.

Farmer's shops

These are found in country towns and have all sorts of equipment from bulk fertilizers and pitch forks to all-weather anoraks at very good prices. Again, you need to be introduced by someone or have a business card you can hand over. Farmer's shops are often found in light industrial areas just outside agricultural towns.

Factory shops

Shopping in a factory shop is often a way of getting an item you want but at direct-from-the-factory prices. Many of the lines in a factory outlet will be between 30 and 70 per cent below what they would sell at in high street stores. The original purpose of factory outlet shopping centres was to help manufacturers clear stock that was out of season, that they hadn't sold enough of on the high street, special orders or overruns. Small, individual factory shops have been common in the UK for well over a century. Most sell womenswear and menswear. Factory shops can sell a particular factory's merchandise, near the actual factory. These are usually very basic, accentuating the 'factory' aspect of the store. Here it is easy to reject the not-quite-right and to pounce on the one or two real bargains you might find. It's sensible to visit fairly regularly as the merchandise changes frequently. There are about 45 factory shopping centres in the UK.

Factory outlet centres and shopping villages

Shopping villages – enormous landscaped shopping areas – are a sort of antidote to online shopping. They vary in character, some being quite basic, others tending towards the 'designer' end of the market, but they will usually include clothes and shoe shops, delicatessens, household products, textiles, furniture, bookshops and plenty of places to play and to eat and drink. They are intended to lure families away from surfing products using their computers in the comfort of their own homes to roaming a physical, landscaped environment for a whole day with the expectation of excellent discounts on many products.

Factory outlet centres are similar in providing a full shopping 'experience' including sports gear, household items, fashion accessories, outdoor clothing and equipment. They are similar to shopping villages but usually much more basic. Many such outlets have become enormous shopping 'malls' with parking for 2,000 vehicles. Obviously they are carefully designed to persuade you to part with your money so it's difficult, even taking the factory prices into account, to be thrifty.

Factory shops in France

In France factory shopping centres have grown quickly in recent years. Last year's stock can be legally discounted for sale at factory shops all year round as well as over-production and discontinued lines. Seconds can be bought as well and these are clearly marked. There are also overstock items from catalogue companies (in France the main ones are La Redoute, Les 3 Suisses, Vertbaudet and Damart). Factory shops worth visiting in France are Roubaix, Troyes and Metz-Talange for glass, Le Creuset for cookware and Villeroy & Boch for table and glassware.

Charity shops

Charity shops are retail outlets selling mainly second-hand donated goods to raise funds for their parent charities. Traditionally, charity shops used to occupy unlet or unpopular shops and some still do that over the Christmas season to sell Christmas cards. The majority are now not only permanent but often in prime trading locations in high streets and market towns. There are now thousands of shops in the UK run by charities for cancer, mental health problems, homeless people, and many more. Many stock clothes, furnishings, toys, ornaments, computer games, bric-a-brac, crockery, bedspreads, CDs and videos no longer available in other stores. Some actually also have furniture and electrical appliances and some open specialist shops such as charity bookshops, bridal wear or music shops. Most goods sold in charity shops are given by the public but some shops do sell 'bought-in' goods. There are often happy surprises to be found such as little-worn designer clothes or genuine 1960s dresses amongst the anoraks and you will often find a good selection of second-hand books.

As charities they benefit from tax concessions so the prices charged are often lower than commercial second-hand shops. But even with charity shops you should shop around because some, such as Oxfam, charge substantially more for their clothes than other charities.

Apart from your own thrifty satisfaction, shopping in a charity shop gives you the extra benefit of knowing you have contributed to some good work. Every year UK charity shops raise more than £100 million for funding medical research, overseas aid, environmental initiatives, supporting sick and deprived children, homeless people, mentally and physically disabled people, animal welfare and many other causes.

Some charities will drop off a bag for people to fill and then pick it up the following week. This is a good way of being thrifty with belongings if not exactly with money. But don't be conned by giving to bogus charities. If it goes in a legitimate charity bag it will help raise funds for that charity, it will provide affordable clothing for those who need it or will find some other useful function.

> NOTE: Bogus charity collections – if a bag turns up with the name of a charity you don't recognize and the explanation is so vague that you become suspicious, throw the bag away and forget it. If you can't find the company registration number on the bag, it's probably bogus. You can phone the Charity Commission on 0845 300 0218 and ask if the charity is legal or bogus. If you have a large number of items you had hoped to get rid of in a good cause, call your local charity shop and see if they will come and collect.

Emmaus is a chain of charity shops with a difference. The idea was born in 1951 by l'Abbé Pierre in France when he started a hostel for impoverished young people which he called Emmaus. His idea, in a nutshell, was that every person, society and nation should exchange and share with dignity. The movement has helped thousands of young people to earn a living and one of the results was a chain of charity shops throughout France selling low priced, second-hand furniture repaired by young people in his workshops. The movement has now spread to 41 countries and it is possible to economically furnish your home from Emmaus branches round the world.

CHARITY SHOP TIPS

▶ *Go to shops in wealthy areas as they tend to have better clothes and more valuable bric-a-brac.*

▶ *Some of the larger, better-known charities have become too knowing about prices and have experts on hand to value antiques. Seek out smaller charity shops that have more to rummage through, usually lower prices and often some pleasant surprises.*

▶ *Check clothes very carefully for stains, moth holes, and other damage.*

▶ *Other people's shoes are not usually good buys.*

Street markets

Local street markets are entertaining, full of variety and offer excellent bargains. Many towns hold a market on one day a week. There are markets that concentrate mainly on food. Every market has a personality and character of its own. For example, one is known for its cheese stall, another for French traders with olives and saucisses, others have shoes made locally or Victorian jewellery.

LONDON MARKETS

London's Camden Passage in Islington has a huge selection of antiques and second-hand clothes, jewellery and bric-a-brac – cheaper nowadays than the better-known Portobello Road market. Columbia Road Flower Market is a Sunday market in East London selling plants and cut flowers – good bargains can be found here, and there are several little gift shops, coffee shops and cafés. Smithfield Market sells meat at wholesale prices. Leadenhall Market (fourteenth century) sells fish at wholesale prices. Borough Market, established in 1756 is London's oldest fresh produce market and still trades from its original site with a really good selection of fresh meat at excellent prices. New Covent Garden Market sells fruit, vegetables and flowers – it's a good place to buy huge quantities of fresh flowers the day before your wedding. Camden Market specializes in cheap clothes at weekends and Portobello Road and Brick Lane sell bric-a-brac at weekends.

Insight

The best-known markets usually up their prices for tourists. They are entertaining and can be good value, but check prices before being carried away by your or their enthusiasm.

Auctions

An auction is a sale of goods or property in which prospective purchasers bid until the highest price is reached. Buying at auction can be a cheap way of acquiring almost anything, provided you don't get carried away by your own enthusiasm. As with haggling, the important thing is to set a limit on how much you are prepared to spend and not to go above it. Almost anything can be sold at auction including antiques, fine art, collectibles, property, furniture, cars and government surplus goods. At auctions remember the following:

▶ *Bidding at auction is a skill, like most shopping, so start by bidding for small, non-valuable items while you learn the ropes.*
▶ *Get a catalogue and study it carefully (but remember items listed may change by the time the bidding starts).*
▶ *Examine the items before bidding. There should be a period when the goods are on show before the actual auction starts.*

Look in local papers and specialist magazines for local auctions. Auction News is a monthly magazine with details of all auctions by official receivers, county courts, Ministry of Defence and the police. Two useful websites in the UK are www.governmentauctionsuk.com, which gives information on auctions of ex-government equipment from houses and cars to furniture and jewellery; www.ukauctionguides.co.uk gives information on auctions and lists of local auctions throughout the UK. Typical goods are laptop computers, office furniture, go-karts, flat-screen televisions, car stereos, cars, motorbikes and HGVs; www.greasbys.co.uk sell London Transport lost property at 26 sales throughout the year. In the USA, www.auctionguide.com is a guide to auctions of all kinds throughout the country.

Buying from a private seller

Insight

Beware when buying expensive items from friends or neighbours. If something goes wrong it's difficult not to blame and the 'culprit' is constantly there to remind you.

When you buy from a private seller, you have fewer rights than if you were buying from a shop or business. Some traders pretend to be private sellers to take advantage of the fact that the buyer has fewer rights. This is illegal and you can contact your local Trading Standards Department if you suspect something untoward is going on.

▶ *Warning signals to look out for if you think the private seller is in fact a trader are if the seller insists on coming to your house; insists on being paid in cash; refuses to give you a receipt and won't give their address.*
▶ *Take someone with you when you are buying privately to support you and act as a witness if necessary.*
▶ *Beware of the 'wet' bargain – something bought from a stranger in a pub over a couple of beers.*

Things the thrifty will avoid

DOOR-TO-DOOR SALESMEN

If someone rings your front doorbell to sell you anything, whether it's religion, a pack of tea towels or solar panels for the roof, your heart usually sinks – and with good reason. This is a form of selling that often targets older people and uses bullying tactics so that people may find themselves signing up to something that will cost more than they can afford for something that will never pay for itself in their lifetime. A man/woman, perhaps with some sort of disability, may arrive with a heavy suitcase full of cheap gloves, dusters, pet-fur removers. They may have some form of identity badge but this is not a good way to help vulnerable people and you should be suspicious of the organization that sends them out with second-rate merchandise to knock on strangers' doors. Theirs is a difficult trade and if one door has opened to them they will call back time and time again in the optimistic hope of making another sale.

Beware of a ruse that can undermine customer rights. Under the law, if a door-to-door salesman makes an unsolicited visit then any contract signed is subject to a seven-day cooling-off period. But if someone delivers leaflets offering a 'free survey' of double glazing, say, and you fall into the trap of ringing them back to arrange a visit, the company has then been 'solicited' by you and can sell its products with no right to cancel. Anyone with concerns about a purchase they have made from a door-to-door salesman may redeem their thrifty status by ringing the Consumer Direct helpline on 08454 040506 or visit www.consumerdirect.gov.uk.

ONE-DAY SALES

One-day sales appear suddenly in a hired local hall offering goods such as 'hand-painted art' or 'Oriental carpets' or huge discounts on brand-named goods at bargain prices. They take place in venues such as a church hall or hotel or an empty shop. They are advertised in local newspapers and by leaflet. Buyers are often not allowed to inspect the goods before the sale nor immediately after they've bought. Goods always turn out to be inferior or counterfeit – sometimes even just empty boxes. The law would theoretically protect you from such goods but it will be almost impossible to track down the holders of such sales. It is difficult to see where the attraction lies in goods that you are not allowed to look at, no matter how low the price and the thrifty will certainly not be interested enough to walk through the doors.

10 THRIFTY SHOPPING TIPS

1 Go to charity and second-hand shops in a smart or wealthy area of town where the clothes will be of high quality and probably hardly worn.

2 Buy cotton dresses at the end of the summer to wear next summer.

3 If you are looking for attractive small pieces of china or glass, car boot sales and charity shops are a good bet.

4 IKEA, an economical place to buy sprightly design in its own right, always has a few special bargain items before Christmas to encourage customers to buy more, for example, shiny red ceramic flower pots, a big bag of tea lights or a set of stacking, coloured, plastic tumblers each for the price of an energy-saving light bulb.

5 Buy your Christmas presents for next year the week after Christmas and your sugar eggs just after Easter when shops are anxious to get rid of them.

6 Go straight out and redeem any vouchers you receive from stores, garden centres and so on before they become out of date. The savings may seem derisory at the time but over a year could be enough to buy you a slap-up dinner.

7 Avoid false bargains such as cheap bathroom scales that tell you the wrong weight or toasters whose element breaks before the first piece of bread is done.

8 When getting new spectacles, get your eyes tested by a high street optician and then buy the actual glasses frames online from only £15 ($22.50), using your prescription.

9 When shopping at jumble sales, market stalls, small shops or car boot sales, if you see something you want, go back

just before closing time when sellers are anxious to get rid of goods. You may have missed your bargain, but that's a risk you may think worthwhile.

10 *Factory shops often have good bargains in bathroom towels and everyday wear such as fleece jackets and T-shirts.*

QUICK REVISION TEST

1 What is the main disadvantage of a store card?

2 What is the advantage of a charity shop over a commercial second-hand shop?

3 If you break something in a shop, do you have to pay for it?

4 What can you expect to benefit from in a farmer's shop?

5 When is the best time to shop for Christmas presents?

8

Reduce, reuse and recycle

In this chapter you will learn:
- *how to recycle or reuse different products and materials*
- *how to salvage discarded objects*
- *about buying products made from sustainable sources.*

A useful way to remind yourself of thrifty opportunities in the home is to remember the three thrifty Rs: Reduce, Reuse and Recycle. It has been estimated that every household produces about one tonne of rubbish each year. In many ways, thrifty living and 'green' living go together since being thrifty with the earth's resources nearly always means being frugal money-wise as well. Much of the thrifty advice about reducing household bills, for example, is as relevant to diminishing your carbon footprint as it is to reducing the household budget.

Recycling is an obvious case in point. There are dozens of ways in which one can recycle or salvage things used every day at home. Local authorities are making it much easier for people to recycle their glass, paper, aluminium and garden waste. There is much unused food, vacuum dust and waste paper that those with gardens can put straight onto the compost heap instead of sending it all to landfill.

But there are many ways to use salvaged and recycled materials and objects apart from actually sending things to the local tip. You probably already put all your glass into recycling bins.

You can also buy and use products made with that recycled glass such as kitchen worktops, glass wall bricks and many other artefacts including recycled tumblers and wine glasses and coloured glass 'gravel' for the garden.

The truly thrifty person will take things much further than that. Before buying anything new for your home get into the habit of asking whether you actually need the object at all. Could you repair or renovate it? Could you use it in some other capacity?

Think long term – buy things with the idea of making them last or using them in some other capacity when you do eventually want to replace them. Many things can be passed on to others who might need them. If you really do need a new item try to buy something made of sustainable materials or consider getting a second-hand one and ask where the materials used in its manufacture come from and how a particular object was made. Does the wood come from sustainable forests? Are those tiles made from recycled glass?

Reducing

Cut down on the amount of 'stuff' that will need recycling in your home. This mounts up rapidly every time you come home and unpack your bags or the postman calls or you open a can of beans. Clutter is the despair of so many homeowners and reducing this is a first priority on the way to thriftiness.

▶ *Don't buy goods with masses of packaging or if you do, leave the packaging at the shop. Legally you are allowed to do this, even if, in practice, it's a bit embarrassing.*
▶ *Prevent junk mail from piling up on your doorstep through the free Mail Preference Service (see Taking it further).*
▶ *Cancel unwanted newspapers and magazine subscriptions – you can always read them in your local library.*

- *Don't build up piles of disposable nappies, keep them for occasional use such as long journeys and use a nappy laundry service.*
- *Only print out information from the internet when absolutely necessary.*
- *Use software such as Fine Print to reduce paper usage by up to 50 per cent.*
- *Use a washable roller towel in the kitchen instead of disposable paper towels. A roller can be fixed to a kitchen door.*
- *At work, encourage your company to buy reusable cups and glasses rather than disposables.*
- *Toys pile up inexorably at home, many seldom played with. Join a toy library so that you can borrow toys and give old ones to other families. Toy libraries can be found throughout the UK and the USA. They are a network of community resources for play which may include equipment, toys for loan, dedicated space and skilled staff.*

Reusing

Many things that get thrown away could be reused many times and there are many ways in which older objects can be repaired, revived and renovated. Furniture can often be refurbished so that it's as good as new or given another life in a different room. Kitchen appliances can often be repaired and reused rather than thrown away. Unfortunately the way goods are packaged, presented and advertised encourages the feeling that things are only worthwhile if they are new and fashionable. However, the thrifty will find satisfaction in finding uses for familiar and battered things.

Paper is both over-used and under-used. We buy far too much, use far too much, throw away far too much and fail to use it economically.

- ▶ *Reuse scrap paper for writing notes or put on the compost heap.*
- ▶ *When printing, use both sides of the paper unless you want to send a formal letter – the paper will last twice as long.*
- ▶ *Reuse envelopes by sticking new labels over the old addresses.*
- ▶ *Buy reconditioned electrical appliances from organizations such as Create.*
- ▶ *Buy your new TV, fridge, washing machine or other white goods from a retailer who will collect your old one for recycling, even if there's a small fee.*
- ▶ *Find new windows for old curtains or exchange them at the Curtain Exchange (see Taking it further).*
- ▶ *Give unwanted tools to charities that send them to developing countries.*
- ▶ *Plastics are often used unnecessarily with serious consequences since most won't biodegrade and end up in landfill sites.*
- ▶ *Remember to take your own reusable shopping bags to the supermarket so you don't stock up on dozens of unwanted plastic bags. Save on disposable cups and plates by renting or borrowing party glasses, cutlery and crockery. Some supermarkets hire out glasses for parties.*
- ▶ *Instead of throwing out old batteries use rechargable ones with a solar powered recharger.*
- ▶ *Shun disposable cameras and buy a proper one instead.*
- ▶ *Buy as much as you can in refillable containers: washing powders, cereals and suchlike are available like this, especially in organic shops.*
- ▶ *Mend, re-upholster or restore and re-paint old furniture instead of buying new.*
- ▶ *Rent or borrow items you don't use very often such as DIY tools rather than buying your own.*
- ▶ *If you can't reuse large pieces of furniture yourself, perhaps your local charity shop will collect them. A few have repair workshops that can renovate and find new homes for old sofas, dining tables and other large items.*

Recycling

Recycling means reusing materials to create new items, reusing
items for a different purpose than the original or sending them
away to be reused by somebody else. There are many ways in
which the thrifty can be highly creative when finding ways to
recycle objects.

▶ *Get your office to recycle vending cups via the Save a Cup
  scheme (see Taking it further).*
▶ *Choose products that are wrapped in packaging you know
  can be recycled. For example, cardboard and crushed paper is
  better than polystyrene chips or peanuts.*
▶ *Turn as much waste as you can into excellent compost. You
  may be surprised at how much of what you throw away can
  actually be composted in the garden.*
▶ *Buy products made from recycled materials.*
▶ *Make the most of your recycling centre. The best ones will
  take building materials, garden clippings, furniture, glass,
  old computers and so on, all sorted into separate areas.*
▶ *Recycle your plastic carrier bags by taking them to a small
  local supermarket or 'eco-friendly' shop.*
▶ *An old container can be filled with straw and set in a quiet
  spot of the garden as a winter home for hedgehogs.*
▶ *Old natural fibre carpets and rugs make good covers for a
  large compost heap and keep the weeds down in the kitchen
  garden.*
▶ *Fibre egg cartons can be turned into papier maché for hours
  of moulding fun or put on the compost heap.*

RECYCLING SYMBOLS

Various 'green' organizations have devised logos indicating that certain waste products are suitable for recycling and that certain other products are made from recycled materials. Look for these logos but be warned, they are not always well-designed or easily identifiable.

1 *Glass: symbol means please put this in a bottle bank.*
2 *Recyclable aluminium.*
3 *Recyclable steel.*
4 *Paper: this mark (given by the National Association of Paper Merchants) means that paper or board must be made from a minimum of 75 per cent genuine waste paper and/or board fibre, no part of which should contain mill-produced waste fibre.*
5 *Plastics: there are seven symbols to identify the type of plastics, resins or multi materials a product is made of.*
6 *Wood: the Forest Stewardship Council (FSC) logo identifies products which contain wood from well-managed forests independently certified in accordance with the rules of the FSC.*

Recycling know-how for specific materials

There are many reasons for recycling. The most thrifty are that if we reuse things we don't have to buy replacements, also that recycled products are often cheaper to buy. Other related reasons are that we are running out of space in landfill sites and many electrical and electronic products release potentially dangerous toxins into the earth when buried in the ground. Rubbish spoils the natural environment and can harm the habitats of wild creatures. Recycling facilities vary wherever you live. Contact your own local authority to find out how they organize their recycling. There are some general principles however, which are useful to know.

PAPER AND CARDBOARD

▶ *Paper recycling is a cost-effective means of acquiring raw material for recycled products. There are over 50 grades of waste paper divided into 11 groups. These groups cover material that can be used for recycled newsprint, tissues and industrial wipes, stationery and packaging.*

▶ *Most types of paper and cardboard are accepted by local recycling schemes: newspaper, magazines, coloured and brown paper, envelopes (including the plastic windows) and junk mail (without plastic wrappers).*

▶ *Why not stop the junk mail altogether by contacting the Mailing Preference service (see Taking it further)?*

▶ *Cardboard packaging can take up a lot of room in the average household rubbish. It is made of cellulose fibres, generally from wood pulp, which can be used again. Cardboard boxes should be flattened as much as possible and should be empty. If you can, remove any adhesive tape.*

▶ *Put old cardboard on the compost heap.*

▶ *Lay cardboard on the ground to frustrate weeds in the kitchen garden or allotment.*

▶ *Use shoe boxes for storage (paint them bright colours).*

▶ *Use cardboard boxes as play structures for your children.*

Insight

Don't forget that a lot of paper and cardboard is suitable for the compost heap. Don't include sticky tape or very glossy paper but paper bags, envelopes and a certain amount of newspaper, can be torn up and mixed well with kitchen peelings and grass cuttings and annual weeds to add substantially to the amount of compost you can achieve.

GLASS

Some authorities may ask you to put different kinds of glass into different containers. It makes economic sense to separate high quality grades from inferior grades.

▶ All bottles and jars are accepted and it helps if they are rinsed with caps and lids removed.
▶ If using bottle banks, do sort bottles into the correct colours because if there is contamination with different colours the quality of the glass is reduced. Blue bottles are classed as green.
▶ A few types of glass are not suitable for recycling because they are manufactured differently (these include toughened glass such as Pyrex, window panes and ornamental glass such as vases).
▶ Glass can be recycled again and again, using less energy in furnaces and fewer raw materials. Recycled glass is made into new bottles and jars, tumblers and wine glasses, coloured 'gravel' for gardens and tiles. It's even used as an aggregate in road building. Glasphalt looks just like any other tarmac but is 30 per cent crushed glass, specially treated so it won't puncture your tyres.
▶ Processed sand is finely ground glass and is used in golf bunkers.

ELECTRICAL ITEMS

It is an offence to put your old refrigerator or freezer out onto the street. Most local authorities will make an appointment to collect if you telephone first and some dealers will remove your old appliance when delivering a new one. Ask before you buy, because this is a very worthwhile service.

MOBILE PHONES

Tens of millions of mobile or cellular telephones are thrown away every year never to be used again. There is growing concern about the serious environmental problem caused by the build-up of these old, obsolete and toxic phones. However, there are plenty of people who could use them so they should be recycled. Most mobile phone batteries are now made from lithium ion which is recovered during the recycling process and put back into productive use. Other battery types are nickel metal hydride batteries. These are also specially treated, the materials recovered being made into things like saucepans, irons and new batteries. So why not donate your old phone? Recycled phones go to people overseas who can't get a regular telephone service. If you are donating fewer than ten phones send them in a Jiffy bag to Oxfam Bring Bring Scheme (see Taking it further). Or take your phones to any Oxfam shop.

COMPUTERS

▶ *Try to give away or recycle your old computer before it becomes completely obsolete. Don't let it sit in a cupboard for several years until you have to recycle rather than donate it. Give it to a local schoolchild or charity or go to www.itforcharities.co.uk which gives information on organizations in the USA, Canada and UK that will take your old computer, refurbish it and pass it on. Electronics contain lead and other chemicals so they should not be sent to landfill sites. Contact your local authority for advice.*
▶ *Some computer manufacturers such as Dell and Apple provide customers with their own recycling programmes.*

FOOD TINS

▶ *These are made of steel coated with a thin layer of tin and can be recycled into more tins, car parts, fridges and other domestic appliances. You don't have to remove the labels as these are fired off during the extremely hot smelting process but you should rinse them before collection. Dirty tins are unhygienic and contamination can disrupt the smelting process.*

ELECTRONICS

▶ Some retailers take back old electrical items when delivering a new one.

▶ If your item still works safely, you could sell it through your local paper, notices in local shops or online.

▶ There are plenty of reuse networks including your local council who can accept items for other people to reuse.

FURNITURE

▶ Don't chuck it out, re-paint it and give it a new life, perhaps in a different room.

▶ Local charity shops, schools and community groups can sometimes use unwanted items although it is sometimes difficult to get anybody to take large pieces of furniture.

▶ If you can't find anybody to give your old furniture to, take it to the tip or perhaps your local authority will take it away for a small fee. If you are over 60 they may remove it for free.

▶ Do you really need a new bed? Why not simply buy a new mattress for the bed you already have? (Mattresses made with foam have to have a kite mark to prove they meet British safety standards, so second-hand foam furniture is not advisable.)

TEXTILES

▶ Old clothes, bedding, curtains and blankets can be recycled on any high street at charity shops but make sure they have been washed or dry-cleaned first.

▶ Some local authorities have recycle bins for textiles and some charities will accept or even collect textiles.

▶ If you deposit shoes, tie them together so they don't get separated.

ALUMINIUM CANS

▶ This is the most valuable of recyclable materials. The energy it takes to make one new aluminium can is enough to make

20 recycled ones as the mining and transport of the
bauxite use large amounts of energy. Aluminium cans are
melted down and turned into ingots of aluminium which
are used to make new cans. This is called closed loop
recycling, because old cans go in and metal to make new
cans comes out.

▶ Cans should be cleaned although you don't have to remove
the labels.

▶ Cash for cans schemes are run all over the UK where
aluminium cans can be exchanged for cash donated to help
raise funds for charities and other good causes. Invest in a can
crusher so they'll take up less garbage space.

▶ How can you tell whether a can is made of aluminium?
Test the side of the can with a magnet. If the magnet does not
stick, it's aluminium.

ALUMINIUM FOIL

▶ Bottle tops, takeaway containers and cooking and wrapping
foil are all accepted by recycling schemes.

▶ Don't include plastic (such as crisp packets). You can easily
tell by squashing the object. Aluminium foil will stay
squashed, whereas the plastic will spring back. Foil should
be washed, squashed together and kept separate in the
recycling box.

SPECTACLES

▶ Unwanted glasses can be taken to Help the Aged stores.

▶ Some local authorities will take spectacles too. The glasses
are sorted and cleaned and then passed on to a charity such as
The World Sight Appeal or Vision Aid Overseas who donate
them to communities in developing countries, particularly
to people who would not otherwise have access to any
professional eye-care.

▶ In the USA, chain stores LensCrafter, For-Eyes and Pearle all
collect glasses.

CAR BATTERIES

▶ Most recycling centres and many garages now have facilities
  to receive car batteries. If the local authority won't collect
  them, you will have to take them to your local tip. Batteries are
  crushed and broken down into valuable component parts which
  are sorted. Plastic is washed, dried and ground up into granules
  used in many different products, including recycling collection
  boxes, furniture, paint trays, car parts, drainpipes and more car
  battery cases. Lead is melted down to make guttering for roofs
  and shields for X-ray machines in hospitals, acid is treated and
  neutralized. Distilled water is purified and used again.

ENGINE OIL

▶ It is said that one litre of oil can pollute a million litres of fresh
  drinking water. Not surprisingly, it is illegal to pour the oil
  away or burn it. You should be able to recycle it through your
  local tip. The Environment Agency has set up a helpline to
  help oil users dispose of oil responsibly.
▶ When recycled, the oil is used in furnaces at power stations,
  for heating tarmac and drying stone in quarries and as an
  alternative to conventional fuels.

PLASTIC

Plastic is a problem because natural processes will never break it
down. Its manufacture requires petrochemicals from oil supplies
which cannot be replaced and involves high-temperature furnaces
and long-distance travel. It is also lightweight, often filled with air
and so can take up enormous amounts of space. Most discarded
plastic is buried in landfill sites but it is valuable and should have
more than one life. Different plastics are made from different
types of polymers. The different types of polymer give the plastics
different characteristics and make them good for different
applications. The 'bottle' types are most suitable for recycling. So
the kind of plastic container used for milk, fizzy drinks, shampoos,
detergents, cleaning fluids is collected.

DO wash your food packaging before putting it in the recycle
bin or bag. If items have to be sorted they should be clean
and hygienic, otherwise they become hazardous to health.

Most councils will not accept plastic film or carrier bags, tubs and
pots or the sort of punnet in which fruit and meat is sold. Other
clear and opaque plastic can be recycled. They are chopped into
flakes, formed into pellets, melted down for manufacture into
various new products but never used for food or drink again. They
may end up as hard surfaces for furniture, flexible drainage pipes or
the high quality fleece produced for outdoor clothes. Plastic bottles
can be taken back to some supermarkets. Bottles should have their
tops removed and then be rinsed and flattened to save space.

NAPPIES

There are different opinions here. Some say there are many good
reasons to choose real nappies others say the amount of heating
used to wash them means real nappies are not necessarily more
economical than disposables. You'll have to make up your own
thrifty mind. Real nappies can reduce the waste in your bin by up
to a half; they will help the environment by reducing the millions of
disposables sent to landfill every day.

▶ *Modern real nappies are fashionable and easy to use. They do
  not need soaking and are easy to wash at 40–60 degrees.*
▶ *The Real Nappy Project in the UK encourages parents,
  nurseries, clinics and hospitals to use washable nappies and
  reduce the volume of disposables going into the waste stream.
  It is run by the Recycling Consortium, an awareness-raising
  not-for-profit organization.*
▶ *Talk to your local authority to see if they have an incentive
  scheme.*
▶ *Try a loan service before you buy (i.e. test a service for a
  period for free).*
▶ *Wash covers, also known as wraps, at 40°C where possible so
  that they last longer.*

- ▶ *Check out prices on internet sites such as eBay.*
- ▶ *Don't buy birth-to-potty packs unless you are sure the nappy system works for your child.*

WOOD

Wood is a problem in landfill sites because it is often bulky and takes a long time to decompose.

- ▶ *If you can, find uses for any wooden planks, shelves, posts that you have at home.*
- ▶ *Scrap wood is usually collected at local authority recycling centres.*
- ▶ *Many local councils now have a service for collecting Christmas trees a few weeks after Christmas.*

Insight
Wooden boards and planks can be used to create raised beds for growing vegetables. As well as thriftily recycling the wood, they make it easier to deal with slugs and snails, as well as being easier to cultivate and harvest.

HAZARDOUS WASTE

Lots of the chemicals and medicines found in the home are highly hazardous. Do not pour chemicals or oil down drains. They can pollute rivers. Old or leftover paints can often be used by local community groups or can be recycled at most civic amenity sites. Plastic bottles that have contained household cleaners can be recycled but check instructions on the bottle.

Medical waste is hazardous too. Dispose of medicines following either your doctor's or the manufacturer's instructions or take them to a chemist. They should not be poured down the drain. Wrap up needles and syringes in layers of newspaper secured with sticky tape. If you find a syringe put it in a safe container and take it to the local police station. Glass bottles and jars that have contained medicines can be put into a bottle bank if they are empty.

Salvaging other people's throw-aways

Other people seem to be incredibly wasteful and spendthrift. You can find all sorts of desirable items thrown into skips or put outside in the street. Anything from sets of perfectly good china to well-designed dolls' houses or functional office chairs. It's always worth pausing if you see things cast aside – perhaps the very thing you have always wanted is sitting there for the asking.

SKIPS

A very good way to find bargains is to glance into any skips you see in the road. Most of the time they are filled with old builders' junk, broken bricks, and so on. But very often they also have bits of wood that can be used as firewood or even shelves. People often use skips to surreptitiously throw away things that really ought to go to the local charity shop and those things can be just what you're looking for. Every skip has been hired by someone for a particular job. If you can find the person who hired the skip, ask whether you can retrieve things from it. Theoretically you are stealing if you take from a skip, although mostly nobody takes much notice, especially if you go about it unobtrusively. You can find chairs, tables, shelving, plumbing discards – often quite usable – as well as all sorts of electrical equipment from TV and stereo parts to whole working computer systems.

Be careful how you negotiate a skip, they can be dangerous and if you get damaged you have only yourself to blame. There may be broken glass, rotting food, nails jutting out of wooden posts, and all kinds of unpleasant items. You retrieve things from skips at your own risk. Take with you a pair of strong waterproof gloves, a first-aid kit, a torch plus a backpack or wheelbarrow to put your booty in.

SALVAGE YARDS

Recycled architectural pieces or building materials can be found in salvage yards. You can find anything from doors to staircases, sculptures, stained glass windows, wood flooring, raised panel doors, electrical and plumbing fixtures, bricks, Victorian cast iron baths and much more. Some items are not particularly cheap but it is possible to find bargains and things that are unobtainable elsewhere.

▶ *Antique timber is desirable because it is fully seasoned and won't warp. This is ideal for floorboards, beams and structural components in a house. Pitch pine and other pines, Scots pine and yellow pine, for example, are virtually always available.*
▶ *There are often interesting pieces from demolition of schools, pubs, factories and other large buildings.*
▶ *Salvo is an online directory of all architectural salvage, reclaimed building materials and antique finds. Salvo puts people with material resources in touch with potential buyers. The Salvo website contains lists of dealers and craftspeople, architectural antiques, garden antiques, reclaimed building materials, higher value stock for sale and wanted, theft alerts and other information. Visit www.salvo.co.uk or www.salvoweb.com.*

Buying recycled or sustainable materials

There are many materials available on the market now which are both sustainable and attractive. When you want to replace flooring, choose comparatively cheap products such as linoleum, cork, rubber and cellulose insulation made from newspapers. Grasses, straw and bamboo also make good alternatives to man-made fibres and so do linen and coir. Avoid tropical hardwoods (including plywood) unless you know they are certified by the Forestry Stewardship Council as being from a sustainable source.

▶ *If replacing floorboards try to find old or reclaimed floorboards that can be reused.*
▶ *Cork can be used on floors or walls and has an insulating quality and warmth underfoot which is particularly friendly and comfortable.*

- Bamboo is another fast-growing and therefore easily renewable resource and is becoming popular as a flooring material and as a silky fabric for clothes.
- European soft woods such as pine and birch plywood should come from a sustainable source. Some manufacturers make a point of using sustainable woods and they are not necessarily more expensive, so ask before you buy.
- New furniture may be made of renewable fibre and timber sources such as coconut, palm, sorghum and bamboo.

WOOD SUBSTITUTES

Insight
Recycled and recyclable materials are becoming much more common so make sure you buy them when you can or at least check them out when comparing prices and designs.

- Durapalm is coconut palm wood. It has a natural pattern and the dark colour of an exotic wood. Coconut-palm plantations produce a tremendous amount of waste in the form of 'retired' trees. The trees produce nuts for 80–100 years, after which they are cut down and replaced with younger, more productive trees. The older trees are now being sourced by timber distributors and some of it is turned into furniture.
- Kirei board is made of sorghum waste. It has a highly textured surface and can be made into chairs and tables, flooring and wall covering.
- Plyboo is plywood made from laminated bamboo strips that have been boiled to remove their starches. Plyboo is being made into furniture in a wide range of prices and styles as well as anything plywood is usually used for.
- Compressed newspaper: there are many uses for the newspapers that pile up in the home. It is compressed under high temperature and held together with a glue. It is supposed to use less water, less energy and produce less air pollution in production than traditional materials with similar properties. It is used to make several products for use in the home

including a type of wallboard with excellent weather resistant properties which is used as a building material; pencils; pelleted, biodegradable pet litter with names like Yesterday's News or Carefresh; lightweight ecological coffins which can carry a person up to 115 kg in weight and up to 6 ft (182 cm) tall. Each tonne of recycled newspaper conserves about 300 cubic yards of landfill space. Compressed paper building products are said to conserve more than 1,370,000 trees each year. All water used to conserve compressed paper products is in a closed loop system which reuses the same water indefinitely.

10 THRIFTY RECYCLING IDEAS

1   Try to avoid buying items which contain large amounts of packaging. Some companies such as removal firms will supply cardboard boxes which they then take back for reuse.

2   Old or unwanted binoculars, telescopes, or tripods in good working order can be donated to the Royal Society for the Protection of Birds (RSPB) where they will be used for conservational or educational projects.

3   Cardboard makes excellent compost. Put it in your compost bin with kitchen and garden waste. It also makes excellent mulch for vegetable beds.

4   Buy returnable glass bottles or refill packs whenever possible.

5   Reuse glass bottles and jars for storing odds and ends or give them to a local jam maker.

6   Reuse plastic bags. Use them as bin and waste paper bin liners and keep some in your pocket or handbag for reuse on your next shopping trip – they take up minimal space.

7   You can recycle some fizzy drink bottles yourself by cutting off the bottoms and using them as drawer tidies for paper clips, earrings, rubber bands or any of those small impossible-to-find items you always need in a hurry.

8   Recycle your inkjet cartridges. Most of them come with a little self-addressed Freepost envelope so all you have to do is bag them up and post them.

9   Flatten cartons, soft cans, biscuit and other boxes before recycling them – they'll take up half the space.

10 Use your old CDs as bird scarers in the garden.

QUICK REVISION TEST

1 What products is recycled glass used for?

2 What are the three thrifty Rs?

3 Name two ways in which you can recycle paper and
   cardboard at home.

4 What should you do with old medicines and syringes?

5 Name five sustainable materials that can be used on floors and
   in furniture at home.

9

Savings on clothes

In this chapter you will learn:
- *how to extend the life of clothes and shoes*
- *about buying clothes thriftily*
- *about saving money on children's clothes.*

Clothes shopping is fraught with difficulties and expense. Fashion is always elusive and you can spend a fortune in the search for the perfect garment that will transform your life. Your children grow so fast it's difficult to keep up with clothes the right size and when they become teenagers they seem to need new clothes every day just to keep up with their friends in the fashion stakes. The thrifty have to be disciplined. One answer is to keep yourself to a set clothes budget – so much a month. This is not just a good idea for adults in a family but for the children too, giving them an opportunity to learn to plan for what they really want.

▶ *When buying clothes, plan a minimum basic wardrobe which you can alter and change by using clever accessories. These are much cheaper to buy than lots of new clothes. Tailored and casual clothes are usually wearable for far longer than frilly, patterned or high fashion designs.*
▶ *Your basic wardrobe should be good quality so the clothes don't look crumpled after the first wear and will wash again and again.*
▶ *Buy most of your clothes as separates. Mixing and matching shirts, trousers, sweaters, skirts and jackets will give you much more variety than a wardrobe full of matching suits.*

▶ *Choose two or three colours that will mix happily so you can vary your wardrobe from day to day.*

▶ *Use tops, scarves, jewellery and hats to alter the look of your clothes completely. A basic, classically cut pair of trousers or jeans can be dressed up or down at will and be completely unrecognizable if worn with different tops.*

▶ *If you feel the urge to buy something new, treat yourself to a new scarf rather than a new dress.*

▶ *Choose non-iron clothes that are washable in cool temperatures. Dry-cleaning is more expensive so best for clothes that only need cleaning occasionally. For example, a silk blouse might need dry-cleaning once a week, whereas you can get away with getting a winter coat dry-cleaned once a year.*

▶ *Seasonal clothes make dressing much more interesting. In winter wrap up warm with extra layers of clothes and lovely all-embracing sweaters. Then you can turn the heating down a notch.*

▶ *Don't hang on to clothes that you haven't worn for the last 12 months. They just get in the way of other clothes, get flung on the floor and are a constant reproach.*

▶ *Once a year go through all your clothes, resolutely throw away those that are stained or damaged beyond repair and donate to a charity shop all those that you never wear.*

Insight

Look for courses in knitting or sewing so that you can create your own garments or alter those you own with confidence. Knitting has become fashionable recently and there are online knitting and sewing clubs and classes you can join.

Getting clothes altered

If clothes need altering when you buy them, the shop may charge for any alterations such as taking up a hem, but your local dry-cleaner probably has someone working in the back who can do such alterations more cheaply as well as put in new zips or linings. This can extend the life of many a useful garment at a very reasonable cost. An old coat can take on an entirely new life if it is given a new lining. (Your dry-cleaner may also know a local tailor who will make up special clothes from paper patterns if you haven't the time or confidence to do it yourself.)

Make your clothes last longer

PROTECTING

Clothes can be made to last twice as long if you look after them well. Those that have spent much of their life crumpled up on the floor will lose their freshness quickly and become fit for nothing but gardening. If a button comes off a shirt, sew it on again at once or you will lose it. Any little unseen tears should be mended immediately to prevent them getting worse. Keep a sewing box so you don't have to hunt around for needles and thread or iron-on patches in emergencies.

Protect all your linen, cotton and woollen clothes against moths. Moths love natural fibres but won't touch synthetics. In the wardrobe, keep special clothes you don't wear often bagged up in special zip-up clothes bags. For clothes you wear and wash or have dry-cleaned frequently this usually isn't necessary but to be on the safe side, hang bay leaves in a muslin bag among the clothes. Other natural moth deterrents you might find around the house include lavender oil, orange peel or a mixture of ground cloves, cinnamon, black pepper and orris root in a muslin bag. You can use moth balls but they do smell very strong. If you store winter clothes in chests during the summer or vice versa, put them into large plastic carrier bags sealed with sticky tape so that moths cannot get in. Carrier bags can also be used for lining drawers.

If you store your clothes in drawers or chests out of season put them away carefully. During the war when materials were scarce and you needed coupons before you could buy them, tights were unheard of and stockings difficult to get, care of clothes was taken very seriously. Here is some rather earnest advice issued by the Board of Trade at the time. We would use tissue paper rather than newspaper today but the instructions are still relevant for the thrifty:

1 *Get your clothes as clean and dust-free as possible before you put them away. Woollen jumpers, sweaters should be carefully washed. Coats, frocks and suits should be thoroughly brushed – dust, dirt and stains attract the moth.*

2 *Mend or patch anything that needs attention and see to loose or missing buttons.*

3 *Tack down pleats, pocket openings and revers, and sew up buttonholes if you want your things to look really well after their rest.*

4 *When hanging heavy garments see that their weight is evenly balanced. Skirts should be hung by two loops from the waistband; notches cut in the hanger will keep them in place.*

5 *Clothes which cannot be hung up should be folded over bunched-up newspaper to prevent creases.*

> NOTE: You may want your warm clothing at short notice so put everything away in the condition in which you would like to wear it.

REPAIR AND REUSE

Some clothes become like old friends. It's unthinkable to get rid of that baggy old sweater even though it's fraying at the sleeves. And why should you? You may no longer be able to wear it on fashionable occasions but it will still keep you warm after a workout at the gym. If there are signs of wear or, horror, moth damage, you can often darn woollen clothes so that the mend is almost invisible. Darning is a forgotten art but it's a great thing to do in front of a boring television programme or sitting over a cup of coffee. You can find tapestry wools in haberdashery shops or departments in many different colours that are fine for mending knitted garments. Worn out areas can be mended with iron-on leather or fabric patches and replacement pockets are available from some haberdashers.

▶ *Sew on buttons of outdoor coats and jackets with buttonhole thread which is stronger than ordinary thread. If you have no haberdashery near you, use dental floss instead which is equally strong. (Dental floss is resilient and fine so it is a good replacement for thread if you are repairing an umbrella, a tent, a rucksack or a string of beads).*

▶ *Put a drop of clear varnish on the thread in buttons which will prevent the thread from unravelling and the buttons from dropping off.*

▶ *Start thinking of any 'new clothes' you want in terms of what you already have. Is there an old item in the back of your clothes cupboard that you could resurrect in a more current style, instead of buying something new? What could you do to make them fashionable and fun to wear again?*

▶ *What do you have that's simply the wrong colour? You could dye it. Better yet, dye a whole bunch of things the same colour, giving you a matching wardrobe. Dyeing clothes can give your old clothes a completely new life. It works well with natural materials such as cotton or linen which take colour well. But remember that different coloured dyes will come out differently on different coloured fabrics. Before you dye anything, it can be helpful to experiment with watercolour paints on paper to see how colours will react together. You can't turn a dark garment into a paler one by dyeing. Make sure there are no stains on the garment – the stained part will react differently with the dye and you will be left with a stain, albeit of a different colour.*

▶ *Add a layer of lace or net to the hem of a skirt to give it new life in the form of a flounce.*

▶ *Transform a plain pair of jeans with a spray of flowers or other decoration sewn on by hand or machine.*

▶ *Disguise a tear or small stain on jeans with a pattern made of several different buttons or patchwork squares.*

RECYCLE

If it really is time to discard old clothes, remove the buttons
and ribbons or anything else which can be reused. A few fancy
clothes can be kept in a drawer and used as dressing-up clothes, or
dismantled to be turned into dolls' clothes, patchwork quilts, and
jeans patches or anything else you may think of. Or turn cotton
clothes into polishing rags but take the time to cut off any seams or
zips so they won't scratch the furniture.

▶ *If you have a garment that you know you want to deconstruct
  for its fabric, take it apart right away even if you don't have
  an idea for what to make from it yet. You can then think of it
  as raw material, full of potential, rather than 'that old dress'.
  It will also take up less space in your cupboard.*

▶ *Keep jeans to cut into small squares to add to a patchwork
  bedcover. Your offspring will probably also want the patch
  pockets to sew together into little bags to decorate with beads
  and embroidery. Keep small bits of anything fine (velvets,
  silks, lace, chiffon or organza) for appliqués.*

▶ *If a garment is too tattered and worn out to sew a practical
  new garment from, use it to make smaller, decorative objects
  (ornaments, sachets, stuffed animals) and/or combine it in
  patchwork with another fabric of a similar weight.*

▶ *Create art overalls for children from adult sweatshirts; simply
  make a slit down the back and add ties. They completely cover
  other clothes and are easily washed.*

▶ *Tie-dyeing white cotton clothes that have become a bit grubby
  but still fit is a fun activity for the family. Make sure it's a nice
  day so you can take the dye outside in case of spills. T-shirts
  can be tie-dyed into desirable 'new' clothes even when they*

are well worn. This is an especially good idea for families with toddlers since whites never stay white for very long.

▶ *Keep a dressing-up box for the family with old scarves, hats, shoes, party clothes and anything else you think could come in useful. You could also keep in it crêpe paper which can be twisted and held in place to create wonderful 'fashions' for special occasions.*

Buying clothes

BUY FEWER

Of course, the thrifty approach when tempted by clothes in shops is to recognize that your wardrobe is already full of jumpers/jackets/skirts/jeans and that any addition will just overstuff the space. However, there are times when something new is really desirable or necessary. Buy good quality for your basic wardrobe. The clothes will pay for themselves in that they will last longer, wash or dry-clean better, take stains less easily, and hang better.

Insight

When the urge comes on you to buy something new for your wardrobe, make it a scarf or other accessory to transform an existing garment or find something in the local charity or second-hand shop instead of your favourite exclusive little boutique.

BUY GOOD QUALITY

A high price in clothes does not guarantee good quality. Good quality is the result of inventive design, intelligent cut and good fabric selection as well as fine sewing. When shopping look for labels telling the fibre content and recommended care; firm, balanced and even stitching; trims that won't date the garment or prevent an otherwise washable garment from being washable; neatly set in zips that glide smoothly; buttons securely stitched on; seams and hems securely finished in suitable yarn.

▶ *Large supermarkets that sell clothes and department stores with 'own label' clothes often have excellent designs and change their stock frequently. They are scrupulously tested in a way that designer clothes often are not.*
▶ *Never buy clothes to wear in anticipation of 'when I've lost weight'.*
▶ *When buying knitted items, choose those that can be laundered in the washing machine.*

CLOTHES FOR SPECIFIC OCCASIONS

For maternity wear, buy 'transition' clothes that you can wear before the bulge shows and which you won't mind wearing again afterwards. Stretch clothes will fit you for most of your pregnancy and still be OK after the baby is born. Most maternity clothes are not cheap and you are not going to wear them forever so buy the minimum and have lots of accessories to cheer them up and alter them for different occasions. Buy several pairs of cheap but comfortable flat shoes in different colours for when you are pregnant. They are better for you than high heels and can be tarted up for special occasions by sticking on sequins or buckles.

Don't spend a fortune on a wedding dress which you'll only wear once. There are so many opportunities to buy beautiful dresses for less including dress agencies, charity shops (some of them have special wedding dress branches) or buy a simple white dress and dress it up for the occasion. The same goes for bridesmaid's dresses. Hiring clothes for the occasion is also an option.

BUYING NATURALLY

If your thrift takes the form of wanting to use natural fibres, there are some additions to the traditional wool, linen, cotton and viscose.

▶ *Hemp and bamboo textiles are available nowadays. Hemp does not need pesticides to be cultivated economically because it is naturally more resistant to pests. Hemp yarns have a quality somewhere between cotton and linen and are often in natural porridge-like colours although more colours are becoming available all the time.*

▶ *Bamboo yarn is said to be stronger than cashmere and stretches more than a silk and cashmere blend. It doesn't pill as easily as synthetic yarns. It is soft and luxurious and is sometimes called 'cashmere from plants'. The manufacturing process is similar to that for rayon. The bamboo stems and leaves are pummelled into a starchy pulp. A finishing treatment transforms the pulp into soft fibres. The bamboo yarn is then bleached and dyed.*

The most difficult thing for manufacturers when using new yarns and fibres is deciding what to put on the care label. With bamboo it is probably best to dry-clean or hand wash the garments and then lay them flat to dry.

LOOKING FOR BARGAINS

Department stores normally offer good quality merchandise, well-known brands and the latest fashions but not low quality products at bargain prices. But they do have seasonal sales with attractive discounts. At these you can get high quality or fashion merchandise at bargain prices.

Seasonal bargains

Insight

Make a note in your diary of upcoming sales and try to get to as many as you can. There may be store sales or special out-of-store fashion sales at any time of year.

Smaller shops may hold sales at any time, particularly closing down sales or clearance of stock sales to make way for the new season's offerings. Department stores are more likely to hold sales at particular times of year. The following calendar gives some suggestions about what to buy in the seasonal sales:

January: excellent time to buy last season's fashions (also household linen, particularly bedding such as sheets, pillowcases, blankets and quilts).

April: after-Easter sales are often good for clothes including men's and boy's suits; men's, women's and children's coats; dressing gowns and women's hats.

July: stores are already thinking beyond summer to their autumn stock and this may be a good time to look for swimsuits, beach clothes and other holiday type clothing.

August: still worth looking for bargains in holiday and beach clothing.

September: if you can wait until after school starts, you can find bargains in school clothes, backpacks and other back-to-school supplies because most people will have bought theirs already.

December: after the 26th you can often find very good bargains in shoes, gloves, scarves – any of the things that people often buy as presents. If you don't want them for yourself, put them in a drawer to give someone on their next birthday or even for next Christmas.

Insight

If you don't enjoy crowded stores during sale time, look for small local shops and boutiques that lower their prices between seasons or after Christmas. They are usually less busy but often offer good bargains.

▶ *In the USA it's worth going to the Thanksgiving Day sale of pre-Christmas merchandise – one of the biggest shopping days of the year. From 26 December through to mid-January there are big after-Christmas sales. This is a really* good moment to buy items that won't date such as gloves or toiletries for next Christmas. In February all the winter merchandise goes on sale and there may be special promotions and clearance sales.

▶ Look in couture second-hand clothes shops. Here you can often buy designer clothes that have hardly been worn and sometimes not worn at all, for prices that are not cheap in themselves but very cheap for what they are.

▶ The Worx designer warehouse sales, started in London's East End in the 1980s, are now hugely successful annual sales. They offer catwalk one-offs and samples from international designer labels, unique items not available elsewhere and current season collections at up to 60 per cent off original prices. The Worx also offers discounts on hundreds of designer brands of clothes at 12 annual sales in London. These include the Designer Women's Wear Warehouse Sale in February and Pre-Christmas Men's Wear Warehouse Sale in December.

▶ London Fashion Week in February ends in a sale of amazing bargains in the tents next to the catwalks. After the catwalk shows have finished you can pay a small entrance fee and gain access to the end-of-season bargains sold off by the various couture houses and small, interesting wholesalers. The reductions are very substantial and the excellent quality items include shoes, boots, bags, jewellery, evening clothes and leather jackets.

▶ Army surplus clothing refers to items once owned by the military which are now surplus to requirements. The army, navy and air force usually dispose of these goods at auction in bulk. Wholesalers specializing in military clothing and equipment buy these and sell them on to retail stores, commonly known as army surplus shops. Examples of items commonly found in British army surplus shops would be jackets, camouflage trousers, army boots, helmets and assault vests. These can be useful for army cadets, service personnel and, some of them, for the general public. Now you can probably more easily buy your army gear online, but do compare sites and prices and check that the items are genuine army surplus.

Miscellaneous tips

▶ Go to an upmarket area to get the best choice of wearable clothes from charity shops. They are often not only better quality but less worn.

▶ Many towns have a clothes-making area. Find the factories and see if they have a small shop for experimental clothes, odd sizes, over-manufacture or out-of-season garments.

▶ At jumble sales, offer to help behind the counter or when collecting. You might then get the chance to buy the best of the bunch before the crowds barge in.

▶ Study the fashion pages in newspapers and magazines to find out where to get the cheap high street lookalikes of haute couture clothes.

▶ Don't buy anything from a mail-order catalogue when it first comes through the door because if you can wait a few weeks, you may get offers of cheaper postage and discounts on the original asking prices.

▶ Clothes hire shops often sell off their used suits and shirts when they are still in good nick. If you want to own rather than hire a dress suit, for example, this might be a good way to acquire one.

▶ Shop online and go through Kelkoo (www.kelkoo.co.uk), for example, which will search for the cheapest prices from several suppliers.

SCHOOLCHILDREN AND TEENAGERS

Insight

Take your children to the cheap clothing chains to shop for clothes where they can buy several garments for the price of one from an expensive outlet. Children grow out of their clothes very quickly and need to replace them often so these shops are a blessing.

▶ Buy colours that can be worn by boys or girls so you can hand them down to the next in line if necessary.

- Buy socks all the same colour, or at least two pairs of the same colour then if you lose some the others will go together.
- Buy plain colours for jackets and jeans which can be paired up with other colours and will be more versatile than patterns.
- For teenage girls, don't shop in expensive department stores; allow them to choose their clothes in stores that specialize in designer clothes at an incredibly low cost. New Look, TK Maxx, Matalan, Primark, Kmart, all specialize in clothes designed for young people, i.e. cheap, fashionable, and short-lived. In a few months a girl will have outgrown her clothes and fashions will have changed anyway. The thing is to drop in from time to time and don't feel you have to buy something every time. Over a year you will find enough bargains to make it worthwhile.
- Get your children involved in the planning and budgeting for their clothes. Encourage them to shop to a budget and to learn to choose for themselves. If you give them a certain amount regularly for clothes they will have to learn to be economical and to save.
- For school, look for generous hems and loose styles so that the child can grow into them and wear them for longer. Elastic waistbands last longer and are more comfortable.
- Children seem to need an inordinate amount of clothes for school. Any way you can save money on these clothes the better. Schools often send out uniform and equipment lists at the end of the school year. This gives you the summer to look for bargain items. If you spread your school purchases throughout the year you can stagger the expense.
- If there is a particular school uniform, see if there's a clothes agency either within the school or nearby that sells second-hand clothes.
- Find out who else's children go to the same school and if they have hand-me-downs from older children.
- If there's no uniform, go for simple sturdy clothes that will withstand wear and washing.

BABY CLOTHES

▶ *Sewing for very young children is not difficult. Learn how to make a few basic pieces and you can make them over and over again in different fabrics and sizes.*

▶ *Choose sleep suits and babygrows without enclosed feet as they will last a baby longer.*

▶ *Buy bargain clothes in end-of-season sales but in sizes your baby will be in six months' time.*

▶ *Buy only easy-care clothes.*

▶ *Swap and exchange baby clothes with family and friends. Good quality clothes can do the rounds and clothe several babies before wearing out.*

Making clothes

Clothes are available cheaply nowadays but if you want something really different and exclusive, using fabric of your own choice, why not try making your own? Because so few people make their own clothes these days many department stores have reduced the fabrics they sell but you can still find cheap and interesting materials in many smaller shops in high streets or even while you are on holiday abroad.

If you have no sewing machine, start with a second-hand, hand-operated one – they are beautifully engineered and there's not much to go wrong with them; they cost nothing in electricity. Alternatively, buy a portable electric model. These are smaller than most, lightweight and a good way to begin if you don't know how you are going to get on with it. Brother sells second-hand machines cheaply.

Once you've mastered the techniques and want to branch out into more ambitious projects you can get a machine that will make buttonholes, do embroidery, patch, oversew, and in fact do practically anything you want it to.

Paper patterns are surprisingly expensive, but once you have bought one you can use it again and again with variations and different fabrics.

▶ *If necessary, take evening classes to get you started.*
▶ *If you have some basic sewing skills, even if you might not want to tackle school trousers or skirts, you could still create a unique pair of pyjamas.*
▶ *Pull apart a well-preserved adult garment to create a fabric to make a child's shirt.*
▶ *If you have a little experience, unpick a worn garment you are fond of, use the pieces as a pattern for a new garment in a different fabric.*
▶ *You can find reasonably priced fabrics in Indian shops, African shops, high street fabric shops and market stalls.*

Insight

Look online for fabrics to ornament or create clothes. There are plenty of individual sellers specializing in, say, Liberty prints or retro clothes and fabrics. Or you may have a fabric shop near you with a good selection of fabrics.

Look after your shoes

▶ *Your shoes will last longer if you wear a different pair on alternate days. This allows them time to dry out and recover from stress.*
▶ *Keep your smart shoes polished. This protects them from getting wet, muddy and cracked. They look better too.*
▶ *If your favourite shoes are getting a little worn, give them a new lease of life with shoe dye which comes in many bright colours.*
▶ *Simple shoes can be turned into party shoes with a bit of paint and glueing on some sequins, beads or ribbons.*
▶ *The life of trainers can be extended with a little duct tape stuck over the soles.*

- *Suede shoes can be difficult to keep clean but old stained shoes can be rubbed with an emery board. Rub the stain lightly with the emery board and then hold the shoe over the steam from a kettle to remove the stain (this works well for suede clothes as well).*
- *If you have no shoe trees, stuff your shoes well with newspaper to help them keep their shape.*
- *Don't put off till tomorrow the repairs that are needed today.*
- *Watch the heels particularly – a run-down heel throws the shoe out of balance and may cause it to wear out before its time.*
- *A make-do-and-mend tip for leather shoes from the Second World War: 'Brown shoes always look well polished if rubbed each morning with the inside skin of a banana. Leave them to dry and then polish them with a piece of dry rag.' (Bananas were not available during the war so it must have been difficult to follow this advice at the time.)*

10 THRIFTY CLOTHING TIPS

1 Hire shops usually sell off their smart suits and shirts while they are still presentable. If you've been invited to several weddings and foresee more, consider buying rather than hiring your wedding gear.

2 Looking for an outfit for a special occasion? Clothes agencies sell hardly worn or never-worn couture clothes at good prices.

3 Buy stretchy maternity clothes which will grow with you during your pregnancy.

4 Buy only easy-care clothes so you won't incur the expense of dry-cleaning.

5 Wait for the sales. Department store sales can be excellent but small individually owned clothes shops also offer good bargains as they try to clear old stock to make way for new in tiny premises.

6 If you know someone in Singapore or Hong Kong, for example, where silk is available and cheap, send them a favourite garment and ask them to get a local tailor to make it up in silk. Prices of both fabric and tailoring are very reasonable; it's the postage that costs but your garment will still be cheap and also unique.

7 Buy plenty of white cotton T-shirts and coloured strappy vests from your local supermarket and wear them as your staple, with a variety of tops and jackets – they are not only cheap but stylish and make excellent polishing cloths afterwards.

8 Learn to darn. This skill can save a frayed or torn, but otherwise serviceable, sweater.

9   *For a new born baby buy the six-month size of babywear.
    You will be inundated with first-size clothes from friends and
    family and babies grow out of those almost immediately and
    you'll be glad of the larger size waiting in the wings.*

10 *Give your old clothes new life by getting them re-lined, re-zipped,
    or shortened at your local dry-cleaners.*

QUICK REVISION TEST

1 *How can you prevent moth damage to clothes and household linen?*

2 *List five natural fibres used for clothes.*

3 *When is the best time to buy bed linen?*

4 *Where can you expect to find cheap fashionable clothes for teenagers?*

5 *How can you remove stains from suede shoes and clothes?*

10

Saving money on food and drink

In this chapter you will learn:
- *where to look for food bargains*
- *about thrifty methods of cooking*
- *how to prepare some simple budget meals.*

Most people have no idea how much they spend on eating so it can be educational to keep a record for one month of every penny you and your family spend on food including supermarket shopping, dining out, fast-food purchases, take-aways, every single packet of crisps or sweets, even just one mini chocolate bar. If you buy-as-you-go when eating – say a cup of coffee and a croissant for breakfast on the way to work, a smoked salmon bagel and a smoothie for lunch in the local sandwich bar and an unfrozen meal in the evening – individually you may not think you are spending a lot, but in fact that is an extremely expensive way to eat. A detailed record of your food expenses can come as a rude but useful shock. Buying a packet of crisps or other fatty or sweet snack is like throwing money away. They have no nutritional value but remove your appetite from the things your body does need.

There are many ways in which you can reduce your food budget significantly. Being thrifty where food and meals are concerned is largely about planning ahead, like so much thrifty thinking. Enormous amounts of food are wasted simply because people have not planned their buying, their storage and their meals sensibly. Do not buy food, however nutritious, if you're not sure when or how you're going to use it. The best strategy is to decide what meals you are going to eat during the next week, make a list of the things you will need and stick to this when shopping. You're less likely to impulse-buy and will therefore save money and waste less food. Having planned your week's meals, you should then make sure you plan the food storage, especially in the fridge or freezer.

Frugal shopping

A KITTY FOR SHARERS

If you're sharing a flat or house with others try organizing a food kitty. This is a way of budgeting with a known amount of money and of making sure you buy sensibly as well as thriftily. You need a few basic rules to prevent arguments:

▶ *Appoint someone to look after the money or take turns monthly.*
▶ *Agree on a certain date each week or month when the money will be collected.*
▶ *Regularly sit down together and agree on a shopping list.*
▶ *Take turns to do the actual shopping – it will take hours if four people have to traipse along to the supermarket every time you need a pint of milk.*
▶ *Appoint someone to be in charge of everyday or top-up groceries.*

SUPERMARKETS

Work out a weekly menu plan to avoid wasting money on 'impulse' buys and unnecessary items. Do one big supermarket shop when your money comes in – once a week or once a month – and stock up on all non-perishable foods. Write a list of what you need for shopping and don't add to it when presented with desirable extras in the supermarket. Make sure you have enough so that even if you run out of fresh food before the next pay day you have enough baked beans and cans of soup to see you through.

Leave the children at home. They will put you under extreme pressure to buy all the things that you have deliberately left off your list of essentials. They will also put you under pressure to finish shopping quickly and go home or on to the swimming pool so you'll find yourself grabbing items without checking the price just to get finished quickly.

Coupons and special offers can save money but they are also invitations to buy things you don't really need or even want. Before taking advantage of an offer find out if the particular product will cost you more than your normal brand even with the coupon. Will you have to drive out of your way to take advantage of the offer? If so, will you save more than you spend on getting there? Own-brand items are often cheaper. They are processed at the same factories as name-brand products but they are cheaper because they are not advertised. Own-brand soups can make an excellent quick snack at lunchtime.

Remember when shopping:

▶ *Find out if there is a food co-op in your area. Co-ops are buying clubs or grocery stores, usually selling locally grown or 'natural' foods to members, often at wholesale prices and sometimes with a share of the profits.*
▶ *Avoid value-added products such as canned tomatoes with herbs – it's cheaper to add a pinch of dried or fresh herbs to a can of ordinary tomatoes.*
▶ *Try to avoid convenience foods. With things like ready-grated cheese and pre-washed vegetables you are paying for someone else to do what you can easily do at home.*
▶ *Cereals are often on offer. Oats and cornflakes are both cheap.*
▶ *Don't buy frozen meals. If you empty the contents of a frozen dinner onto a plate you will quickly see that you are getting very little food for your money.*
▶ *Frozen prawns can be good value for money as they are often on offer. They are particularly handy for stir-fries.*
▶ *Look in the bargain racks. Foods that are just about to go past their sell-by date are sold cheaply there and you may find dented cans (dented is OK, bulging outwards is not).*

▶ *Instead of buying lots of different desserts, buy the ingredients to make a pudding or a cake.*

LOCAL SHOPS AND SPECIALIST SHOPS

Insight

The temptation in supermarkets is to pop into your trolley odd things that catch your eye as well as the items on your list. Do not be tempted! If you only want a few everyday items, go to your local shops.

Don't always rely just on supermarkets. Hunt around for shops that are cheaper and for bargains wherever you are. Your local general shop may have a small choice but very low prices because the local customers can't afford more. Asian, Greek and African owners often specialize in vegetables and other products from their own country which are difficult to find and more expensive elsewhere.

▶ *Shop in small local grocery stores or markets (not delicatessens) in unfashionable areas where food is basic but cheap.*
▶ *Choose loose rather than pre-packed fruits, vegetables and salads. They are often much cheaper than packaged ones.*
▶ *Your local butcher may offer discounts for fresh meat if you buy in bulk and even cut it up ready for freezing.*

STRAIGHT FROM THE FARM

▶ *Many farms run pick your own schemes and this is by no means just for strawberries. If you hunt around you can find pick your own crops all year round from beetroots and blueberries to fennel, beans, peas, greengages, courgettes and cucumbers. This can turn out to be about half the cost of buying the same items in supermarkets. Go to the farthest part of the field where the best fruit will not already have been picked.*
▶ *Once-a-week farmers' markets are becoming quite common in many towns and cities. Local farmers bring their produce up to town. This may include meat,*

vegetables and fruit, home-made breads and preserves.
They are not always cheap but some of the merchandise is.
The products are not necessarily organic and not always
cheaper than you'd find in a supermarket but they are
unique, local and fresh.

▶ In country areas, farms often sell produce at the door, for
example, potatoes by the sack and fresh eggs.

▶ Organic boxes delivered to your door are also now quite
common in the UK and can save money if you do a fair
amount of cooking. You sometimes have to be inventive
because you won't always know what you are going to get
each week. Although they are often thought to be expensive,
if you compare what your box contains with how much you
would pay for the same items from a supermarket you might
be pleasantly surprised.

STREET AND COVERED MARKETS

Insight

Check out your local markets. Some are well worth visiting
once a week. Some are known for a particular type of
product, such as the market in St Albans which was always
known for its excellent cheese stall.

▶ Buy fresh vegetables and fruit from markets not supermarkets.
They are almost always cheaper.

▶ Visit your market at packing up time. Not only will produce
be reduced but you might even find the odd cauliflower or
cabbage that has rolled into the road and if you swoop
quickly enough you could snatch it up for free.

▶ Ask in shops and markets for old vegetables, bruised avocados,
black bananas. Say it's 'for the goats' or 'for the rabbits',
if you're too embarrassed to say it's for yourself.

WHOLESALE MARKETS

In London there are several wholesale food markets where the
general public can find bargains.

- Smithfield market, selling meat at wholesale prices, is one of the few historic markets that has not moved in hundreds of years.
- Billingsgate Fish Market in the East End dates back to the fourteenth century and fishmongers, butchers and grocers still sell produce here at wholesale prices.
- Borough Market, established in 1756, still trades from its original site with a really good selection of fresh meat at excellent prices.

CASH-AND-CARRY SHOPS

Cash-and-carry shops are wholesalers who supply small corner grocery stores and offer big discounts for bulk. You will need to apply in advance or be introduced by someone who already shops there and you may need a business card and a VAT number. Find out beforehand. If you do get permission to shop in your local cash-and-carry remember that you will have to add VAT to the prices on the labels.

- Bulk buying can offer genuine savings, especially if you share out the produce among friends and neighbours. When you get home unpack perishables and wrap them up again into smaller quantities. Check that you will have somewhere to store your items such as a space under the stairs or a broom cupboard.
- Sacks of rice are incredibly cheap from Asian grocers, simply divide up the sack and the cost amongst friends to make substantial savings.
- Concentrate on non-perishable items such as toilet paper, which could be stored in the garage whereas a large box of chicken wings can't.
- Don't be tempted to buy lots of items because they are new to you or exciting. Take your list with you and buy what's on it. Note any other items for next time you go to the cash-and-carry. You can get good savings on boxes of fruit juice; packets of baby wipes; big packages of steaks or chicken thighs, which can be divided into daily portions and frozen until you are ready to use them.

- Skimmed milk powder can be bought in large tins and makes up a milk equal to the protein value of fresh and costs less. Don't use it for babies or young children because many of the nutrients contained naturally in milk are removed during the drying process.
- Pulses are good bought in bulk because they store well and are usually cheaper.
- You can make substantial savings on meat, icecream and vegetables bought for the freezer.

FORAGING FOR FOOD

Insight

If you don't recognize what's edible in the wild, there are books and online advice as well as courses to help you, If in doubt, ask someone who does know. Things to look out for are blackberries, elderberries, sorrel and fungi – but do your homework first.

Plenty of useful plants can be found growing wild, even in the garden. These include dandelions, whose young leaves can be added to salads, and nettles, which make a nutritious soup. Blackberries grow as weeds in gardens and wild in the countryside. They are best cooked together with apples in crumbles and pies. Elderberries are common wild trees whose flowers can be made into fritters or elderflower 'champagne'. Another delicious soup ingredient to pick from the wild is sorrel. Be sure you know how to recognize the plant you are collecting.

- At the end of a market day, when everybody's packing up, you may find quite a number of vegetables that have rolled into the street. Escaped fruit is not so good because it gets bruised too easily but things like cauliflowers, leeks and cabbages can be invaluable.
- Even the tiniest garden can support some food crop even if it's just herbs. Parsley, chives, sage, coriander, rosemary and thyme are easy to grow and good to include in your cooking.

- On a patio you can grow several types of fruit in containers from figs to peaches or blueberries, not to mention vegetables such as potatoes, cucumbers, beans and courgettes.
- Rhubarb is a stately garden plant and will provide the filling for pies and tarts all summer.
- Everlasting spinach, ruby chard and sorrel are all easy to grow in the garden and will give you fresh greens pretty well all year round.

Frugal storage

Insight

Try to clean out the fridge once a week – put any new food at the back and food that needs to be eaten quickly at the front. That way you'll waste less.

Careless storage wastes food. Before unpacking your weekly shop, clear out the fridge and sort out what has to be eaten at once. Put those things at the front so that they'll get eaten first, and the latest purchases at the back. If you get an organic box of vegetables or salad, wash the items and put them loosely in paper bags or 'stayfresh' bags: they will then last well and be immediately ready for use.

LEFTOVERS

- Put leftovers in the freezer if you won't have an opportunity to use them quickly so they're still usable when you need them.
- Freeze leftover tomato sauce in an ice cube tray, then pop the cubes out into a storage bag. Use just a couple of cubes for a one-person batch of spaghetti.
- Don't throw out leftover Yorkshire pudding, steam it the following day and serve as a dessert with golden or maple syrup.
- Put unused mushrooms loosely in an uncovered bowl in the fridge. They will last for days.

Frugal cooking

Insight

You can enliven any soup with herbs to give it a fresh taste. Coriander is an excellent addition to any vegetable soup; parsley, a little thyme or some mint can also add something fresh and different.

Any dish you make at home is cheaper than one you buy ready-made. By choosing economical ingredients you can make cooking at home even cheaper. There are some things it is so easy to make that it makes no sense to buy these anyway, such as Bolognese sauce, French dressing, lentil soup, leek and potato soup.

Keep sweet biscuits, cakes and sweets for special occasions because they are expensive and not particularly satisfying. When you do want something sweet, try fruit buns, scones, fruit itself, malt loaf, low-fat yoghurt or banana custard and eat them as puddings. Nuts and seeds are a good source of protein and healthy alternatives to sweets and crisps, which may give you energy in the short run but encourage you to feel hungry for more soon afterwards. A few seeds or crushed nuts sprinkled over your meal once or twice a week will give you extra nutrients without breaking the bank. Include cheap, filling foods at every meal.

Whole foods such as wholemeal bread, brown rice and pasta are more filling than processed foods. They are just as cheap and release energy more slowly so you don't get hungry so quickly. Wholewheat pasta is cheap and filling and especially thrifty if you make your own sauce rather than buy expensive ready-made ones. Chinese noodles and supermarket spaghetti are incredibly cheap. They cook in about two minutes so are perfect for those who don't have much time or are starving.

▶ *Make your own bread. If you eat a lot you could justify the cost of an electric bread-maker.*

- Porridge is really filling – a great breakfast food and cheap. Oats are another slow-releasing energy food which means you'll feel satisfied for longer and less likely to snack.
- Potatoes are nutritious carbohydrates. Include a few potatoes as part of your vegetables but don't have too many at one go.
- Beans are nourishing, filling, versatile and economical. The cheapest way to buy them is dried. You then soak the required quantity overnight and boil them the next day. Black-eye beans and lentils are the quickest to cook (lentils don't need to be pre-soaked). They can be used to bulk out casseroles, soups, pasta sauces, curries, chilli, pasties and salads. Baked beans are a student staple for a reason – they're cheap and nutritious. Lentils are also very cheap to buy and can be added to a soup or a stew to make a healthier meal – just bear in mind that they take about 15 minutes to cook.
- When buying fruit and vegetables by all means keep an eye out for what is in season but only buy if they are reasonably priced. Theoretically, seasonal products should be cheaper and they will certainly taste better but buying things available cheaply all year, such as bananas and carrots, is even better value.
- Steam several vegetables in the same saucepan so you only have to heat up one pan. No steamer? Use a metal sieve or a colander over a saucepan with a lid on the top.
- Frozen and tinned fruit and vegetables are invaluable as they are cheap, nutritious, pre-prepared and will last longer than fresh. You will waste less as you only use what you want before saving the rest.
- Dairy foods are good value for money. Milk is full of calcium and vitamins; yoghurts can be fairly cheap depending on the brand and make a nourishing alternative to other puddings. Cheese is full of protein but also full of fat so eat it grated which makes a little look like a lot. Hard cheese is cheaper than spreads or slices.
- Don't underestimate good old eggs for a healthy, filling meal.

> **Insight**
>
> Tinned fish can be added to pasta or to rice for a tasty and nutritious risotto. Plenty of herbs such as parsley or coriander will add to its interest.

▶ *Lean meat may cost more but has much better nutritional value than fatty cuts.*

▶ *Buy less meat and bulk it out with beans, rice or potatoes.*

▶ *Chicken and turkey are the leanest forms of meat. Turkey mince contains less fat than other meats and costs about half the price.*

▶ *Meat tends to be better value when bought in larger quantities so look out for 'two-for-one' offers.*

▶ *Liver is cheap, nutritious and easy to cook. Try casseroling it with sliced onions and tinned tomatoes. Serve with mashed potato.*

▶ *Bacon is a good way to start the day, giving you energy for several hours.*

▶ *Soya mince is a lot cheaper than meat minces, and a good source of protein.*

▶ *Use the cheaper cuts of chicken such as thighs or wings when making curries and casseroles.*

▶ *Tinned fish such as sardines, tuna and mackerel are cheaper than fresh, last longer and are easily stored and prepared. Tinned mackerel in tomato sauce, for example, costs very little and makes a healthy snack.*

DRINKS

▶ *The wine and other drinks you buy in a restaurant are more than twice what they would be if you were to drink them at home.*

▶ *Drink tap water rather than expensive bottled water, this also solves the added problem of what to do with the bottles.*

▶ *Don't buy fizzy or sweetened drinks. Children brought up to drink water as their usual thirst-quencher often prefer it to other drinks and it is healthier for them.*

- *Make your own refreshing drink by adding a slice of lemon, lime or some mint leaves to a jug of water. Refrigerate and add a few ice cubes.*
- *Stave off a hangover by drinking a large glass of water before going to bed.*
- *Take to herbal tea made with fresh mint leaves picked from the garden.*
- *Reduce your beer consumption which gobbles up cash and creates a pot belly.*
- *If you do enjoy a beer though, join a beer brewer's club and make your own.*
- *Drink coffee at home not in a coffee bar.*
- *Pour any undrunk wine into an ice cube tray and freeze it to add later to sauces and casseroles.*

COOKING METHODS

Use your oven as little as possible. If you are going to cook a cake or a stew make use of the heat by filling the rest of the oven space with baked potatoes or any other roasting or baking you have in mind that you can then freeze. There are various cooking devices that are cheaper to use than conventional ovens.

- *Apart from their obvious uses as defrosters for ready-meals, microwaves can be used to cook baked potatoes, bacon, casseroles, chicken, meat and vegetables with a minimum amount of time, mess or electricity.*
- *If you cook in your microwave instead of ordering a take-away, you can save a lot of money.*
- *A microwave is particularly useful in a shared kitchen where several people may want to cook at different times. A couple of potatoes and a tin of baked beans is enough to make you a nutritious, filling, quick and economical meal in a microwave.*
- *A pressure cooker will cook cheaper cuts of meat quickly and improve their texture, saving on fuel and shopping bills.*
- *Alternatively, get a slow cooker. Cheaper cuts of meat typically need to cook for longer and a slow cooker does just that without using enormous amounts of electricity.*

- ▶ *A toaster uses less electricity than a grill.*
- ▶ *'Hay box' cookery is the most frugal way to cook soup, a casserole or porridge. In this you get the food simmering in the pan, then put it quickly into an insulated box and let its own heat continue the cooking for several hours. You can cook porridge overnight this way or the evening meal during the day. To make a hay box you tightly pack a wooden box with straw, hay or polystyrene granules, leaving a pan-sized space in the packing. When the pan is simmering, place it in the box, cover with more insulating material and leave for several hours. The initial cooking is essential to kill any organisms in the food. The only energy used for this kind of cooking is the original preparation of the dish such as sautéing and bringing to a simmer. The rest of the cooking is purely due to retention of the heat.*

Some budget meal ideas

EATING OUT

- ▶ *Avoid eating out: meals you prepare at home are usually significantly less expensive than meals you pay someone else to prepare.*
- ▶ *Don't split the bill equally if you go out to eat with a large group of friends. You may eat as thriftily as you like but you'll find yourself subsidizing those who chose the expensive items.*
- ▶ *Save lots of money by eating in bring-your-own-wine restaurants.*
- ▶ *Look out for special offers for meals in specific restaurants publicized in newspapers. Cut out the coupon and show it to the restaurant before you start your meal.*
- ▶ *If you're going to the theatre see if you can get a combined ticket and pre-show meal deal.*
- ▶ *Take the two-course meal for a discount. Usually this means you can have a first and main course or a main course and dessert.*

Insights

Keep several lemons in the kitchen and add some of their juice to dishes, both savoury and sweet, to add to the flavour something subtle, fresh and delicious.

▶ *Convenience foods such as ready sauces can be cheap but are often more expensive than if you were to make them yourself. Bottled French dressing, for example, is very expensive compared with pouring your own oil and lemon juice into a jar and shaking it. Puréeing your own baby food is also usually much cheaper than buying it in jars.*

▶ *Make double portions and freeze one so that you build up a good stock of meals in the freezer for later in the month.*

▶ *The highest cost item in many people's diets is almost certainly meat. Introduce your family to at least one vegetarian lasagne or moussaka a week, say.*

▶ *Make meat go further by mixing beans with mince and other meat dishes. This increases fibre, reduces fat and makes the meat go further. (For example, try putting baked beans in shepherd's pie, kidney beans in chilli con carne, baked beans and garden peas in stews.)*

▶ *Stir frying is a good way to use up the last of your fresh vegetables (anything from carrots, onions, spring onions, celery, French beans or runner beans, tomatoes, broccoli, Swiss chard) plus some chicken pieces or prawns. It's easy, quick and only needs one pan.*

▶ *While you're cooking, make a substantial amount of a cheap meat sauce and refrigerate it and freeze a portion to provide yourself with three separate and varied meals. A tasty mince recipe, for example, can be turned into a savoury mince dish with oven chips, a spaghetti Bolognese and a cottage pie with mashed potatoes.*

▶ *Make a fairly large quantity of traditional French or vinaigrette dressing, keep it in a jar and use it as required. This will cost about half what you would pay in a shop and taste better too.*

Some budget recipes

Basic frugal mince recipe
Amounts according to taste, pocket and how many people you are cooking for

Minced meat
Onions, sliced
Garlic, chopped
Frozen vegetables
Tinned tomatoes
Herbs such as parsley and thyme, chopped
Spices to taste
Salt and pepper

Fry the onions and garlic together with the spices in very little oil until soft but not brown. Remove from the pan and place in a bowl. Fry the mince over a low heat (there's no need to add oil). Drain off any fat from the mince or allow it to cool so the fat can be skimmed off. Steam or microwave the frozen vegetables. Add onions, garlic, spices, herbs, frozen vegetables and tinned tomatoes. Heat everything through and serve with pasta, rice, potatoes or bread.

Insight
Make the most of your freezer by cooking double quantities of mince, stew, lasagne and sauces. Eat half and freeze half. Then you always have something cheap and nutritious to eat when you are hungry or have unexpected visitors.

Versatile rice meal
Boil some rice in a large saucepan. In another saucepan heat some oil and fry chopped bacon rashers, onions, mushrooms and sweetcorn. Add pepper, dried herbs and a stock cube. Drain rice. Mix all ingredients together. This dish can be varied by using different vegetables and chicken or turkey pieces instead of bacon or shellfish such as prawns. You can add soy sauce or stir-fry sauce. If you've made a huge amount, eat half and freeze half.

Ideas for packed lunches

- ▶ Wrap some seasoned chicken or turkey in a leaf or two of red lettuce. Add a piece of fruit.
- ▶ Fill celery sticks with cream or curd cheese or nut butter and wrap in cling film.
- ▶ Spread wholemeal rolls with cream cheese and fill with sliced banana and a drizzle of honey.
- ▶ Pack a selection of raw vegetables such as carrots, broccoli, peppers and celery cut into sticks with a container of cottage cheese or goat's cheese as a dip.
- ▶ Season a pot of plain yoghurt with chopped nuts and enjoy with a piece of crunchy fruit.
- ▶ Bake a sweet potato and sprinkle with cinnamon or nutmeg.
- ▶ Chop an apple into a mashed can of tuna and eat it with celery sticks, carrots, pepper and cauliflower florets.
- ▶ Wrap a few slices of lean ham in lettuce leaves for a crunchy mid-morning snack.

10 TIPS ON THRIFTY EATING

1 *Never food shop when you're hungry. Suddenly you'll be a lot less fussy, the plan will go out of the window and you'll want to buy everything in sight (especially sweet or fatty snacks).*

2 *If you need bread or newspapers, send someone who hates shopping then nobody will be tempted to get a box of chocolates at the same time.*

3 *Don't buy an enormous fridge or freezer unless you have a large family. It will be expensive to run and expensive to keep filled up. Empty fridge and freezer compartments waste electricity.*

4 *Write a list before you go shopping and stick to it – no extra packets of crisps, expensively priced jelly desserts or chocolate bars.*

5 *Share the cost of cheaper bulk buying with another family.*

6 *Throw nothing away – use any leftovers in soups or stir-frys.*

7 *Fill up on economical wholemeal bread, pasta, or rice and add a tasty sauce and just a little meat or fish.*

8 *Take a packed lunch to work instead of buying an expensive bagel and smoothie in a sandwich bar.*

9 *Don't go without breakfast. A bowl of muesli, cereal or baked beans on toast and an apple will keep you going and prevent expensive snacking later on.*

10 *Think of meat as a side dish. Asian food such as a Chinese-style stir-fry uses little meat and lots of vegetables plus noodles or rice. Such meals are nutritious, satisfying and delicious and very easy to prepare with little mess.*

QUICK REVISION TEST

1 *Name five items to be avoided in supermarkets.*

2 *Name five economical items to buy in bulk.*

3 *What can you do with half a bottle of undrunk wine?*

4 *What are the most filling forms of rice, bread and pasta?*

5 *What is hay box cooking?*

11

Thrift in the home

In this chapter you will learn:
- **how to avoid expensive chemical cleaners**
- **how to maintain a thrifty home**
- **about thrifty ways to enjoy your free time.**

There are many opportunities to run your home smoothly and thriftily which won't make life more complicated but which will save money and possibly time. For a start there are the edible cleaners that are already to be found in your home which can take the place of most chemical cleaners. There are many frugal ways of providing good-looking curtains, bedcovers and other soft furnishings without breaking the bank and there are ways of coping with children without buying ever more expensive toys. You can save money by knowing how to deal with builders, how to use your kitchen, how to recycle clutter, how to entertain your children. The home in fact offers innumerable opportunities for saving and having fun while doing so. The frugal should know about Lakeland, a catalogue of invaluable products for household use ranging from cleaning products and cloths to a tabletop cooker that will casserole, grill or toast food using the minimum amount of electricity.

Edible cleaners

The chemicals used in household cleaners are often toxic and usually expensive. Most people are very wasteful in the amount of cleaning products and detergents they use in general. In most cases less is best – and, of course, the product will last longer as well.

You can save a lot of money simply by using 'edible' cleaners, in other words cleaners that you will find in your food cupboard. They are non-toxic, inexpensive but effective and a pleasure to use. There is nothing wrong with using more drastic cleaners if you have moved into a house which is really dirty or for a once-a-year spring clean but for normal day-to-day cleaning edible cleaners are great.

Insight

Proprietary cleaners can be useful if you want to clean up a really dirty kitchen or bathroom but should not be necessary for day-to-day cleaning, when 'edible' cleaners will do the job perfectly well.

Beer

▶ *A traditional method for cleaning oak and mahogany is to wipe with a cloth dipped in warm beer.*

Bicarbonate of soda (baking soda)

▶ *To clean an oven sprinkle bicarbonate of soda on the walls and floor while the oven is still warm from cooking, leave for an hour, then wipe clean.*
▶ *Sprinkle baking soda liberally into smelly trainers and leave it overnight. Shake out the powder in the morning, when it will have absorbed most of the smell.*
▶ *Add a teaspoon of bicarbonate of soda to your laundry for extra whitening.*
▶ *Use baking soda on a damp cloth instead of cream cleaners.*

Bread

▶ A bread ball will remove greasy marks from amber or jet jewellery.

▶ Use bread rolled into balls to clean greasy finger marks off non-washable wallpaper. Cut off the crusts so you won't scratch the paper.

Coffee grounds

▶ Dry coffee grounds on a baking sheet and put them in a bowl in your refrigerator or freezer or rub them on your hands to get rid of food preparation smells.

▶ Sprinkle old grounds around places you don't want ants or on the ant heaps themselves. Used grounds are also supposed to repel snails and slugs.

▶ Steep grounds in water and apply a little of the liquid to furniture scratches with a cotton bud/swab.

▶ Steep grounds in hot water to make a brown dye for fabric, paper or Easter egg painting.

▶ Grounds are slightly abrasive so can be used as a scouring agent for grimy pans.

▶ Grounds mixed with orange peel are supposed to keep cats from using your garden as their lavatory.

Milk

▶ Use a little milk on a cloth to give a sheen to a slate floor.

▶ Remove fly specks from picture and photograph frames with a cloth dipped in skimmed milk.

Oils

▶ Protect ivory, bone and horn with a coat of almond oil.

▶ A little lemon oil applied to slate after it has been washed gives it a lustrous finish.

▶ If you spill alcohol on polished furniture, wipe up the liquid immediately and rub the area with your hand. The oil in your hand will help to restore some of that taken out of the wood by the alcohol.

▶ Rub a scratch mark on a polished table top with the cut part of a Brazil nut or chopped up hazelnuts. They won't remove scratches but the oil will conceal them effectively.

Raw onion

▶ Remove stains from gilded frames by dabbing the surface gently with a cut raw onion.

Tea

▶ A handful of used tea leaves in vinegar shaken in a vase will help remove stains. (No tea leaves? Try grated raw potato instead.)

▶ Wipe hard specks such as fly spots off walls or picture frames with warm tea.

Vinegar and lemon juice

Insight

Lemons are invaluable for cleaning windows, microwaves, sinks, hard water scale, the rough skin of your elbows and your hands. What's more, what's left can be put on the compost heap.

▶ Vinegar and lemon juice are mild acids. Both will clean surfaces such as glass without creating the smears that many proprietary window cleaners do.

▶ Use vinegar instead of a proprietary toilet cleaner. Leave it in the toilet for an hour or so and then flush.

▶ A bucket of warm water with an egg cupful of vinegar and a squirt of washing up liquid will clean most windows perfectly. Wipe the cleaned window with newspaper to get a really professional finish.

▶ Shine the inside and outside of a stainless steel pan by rubbing with lemon juice or vinegar on a cloth.

▶ Fill a spray bottle with half vinegar and half water to make a good mirror cleaner.

▶ Remove greasy marks on antique furniture with a chamois leather wrung out in vinegar and water (15 ml [1 tbsp] vinegar to 300 ml [1/2 pt] water). Dry well.

- *Remove hard water deposits from taps with a cloth dipped in vinegar. If the scale has really taken a hold, pour a little vinegar into a small plastic bag and tie it to the tap for about two hours so the vinegar has time to work.*
- *A tablespoon of vinegar instead of liquid detergent in washing up water helps to remove grease.*
- *Clean glass tabletops with vinegar and dry with paper kitchen towels. Buff up with newspaper.*
- *Clean marble with lemon juice or vinegar but leave it on only for a minute or two. Repeat if necessary but don't leave it to soak.*
- *Clean your microwave oven by standing a dish of hot water in it. Add a slice of lemon and heat the water in the oven until plenty of steam is produced. Then wipe over the interior with a damp cloth.*

Worcester sauce/tomato ketchup
- *These are both good for cleaning up brass and copper – useful for cheap jewellery but don't use them on precious or semi-precious stones or anything particularly valuable.*

Laundry thrift

Insight

Do use the economy wash on your washing machine for everyday washing of clothes. You may occasionally want to use a hot wash for tea towels, bedlinen and very dirty whites but this should only be occasional.

There are plenty of thrifty laundry possibilities. The first rule is to wash less. Laundering uses up a lot of water and a lot of electricity to heat that water and energize the machine. Is it really important to wash coloured T-shirts after every wearing?

Could you not get children's socks to last for two days rather than just one?

Cold water detergents are just as good as hot water detergents and save on energy. Most clothes don't need to be washed at a high temperature and you can save a lot of energy by washing cooler.

Don't buy a tumble dryer – or give away the one you have. Tumble dryers use an inordinate amount of energy and shorten the lives of your clothes. The elastic in underwear and socks, for example, soon gets destroyed. Tumble dryers also set stains and the constant friction is liable to shrink clothes. Get a washing machine with a really good spin dryer and your clothes won't need much more drying anyway. Drying on a line or an indoor drying rack is free.

▶ *Use enzyme-free detergents with few additives and no perfumes.*
▶ *Save money by not using fabric conditioners, particularly not on babies' nappies or clothes worn by people with sensitive skins.*
▶ *Soaking in warm or cold water before washing is the most economical way to get rid of stubborn dirt and stains. You can then wash the items at low temperature instead of a hot wash.*
▶ *Unless your clothes are very dirty use half the recommended amount of laundry detergent.*
▶ *Dry your washing in the sun if you can, as this has a (free) bleaching effect.*

Thrift in the kitchen

▶ *Switch off kitchen appliances at the wall before going to bed at night. After all, do you really need to use the oven or microwave as a clock? A battery-powered wall clock uses less power.*
▶ *Large, decorative food tins can have an afterlife as storage jars for tea, coffee and other dry items. Several tall Amaretti biscuit tins, for example, will eventually make an attractive matching set.*
▶ *Cut down on the use of kitchen and bathroom fans in winter. These fans cool the air and waste household heat. If you want*

to get rid of smells, try growing a spider plant (Chlolphytum comosum) in the room. Other plants that help clean the air include: Musa cavendishii (dwarf banana) and Sanseveria (snakeplant).

▶ Switch off the oven, hotplates and iron a few minutes before you need to stop using them as they use more power than anything else in the kitchen. They will remain hot for some time.

▶ If you are next to your electric kettle when it boils, switch it off by hand. The automatic cut off will leave it boiling unnecessarily long otherwise.

Insight

You may think the kettle advice is a bit drastic but kettles use a lot of energy to heat up and think how often you boil up a kettle to make a cup of tea or coffee during the day.

▶ Cover pots and pans when heating liquids, they will boil much more quickly. Be sure they are the right size for the rings. Any uncovered area of ring will simply be wasting heat.

▶ Thaw frozen meals to almost room temperature before cooking.

▶ Don't open the oven often to check food while it is cooking. You lose 20–50 per cent of the heat each time you do and slow down the cooking process into the bargain.

▶ Never use your oven or hotplates to heat the kitchen. It's a very inefficient way of trying to get warm and is also dangerous.

▶ Don't be persuaded to buy a warranty with any electrical appliance. In the UK you are already protected by consumer laws.

▶ If your stainless steel sink looks dull or splotchy, a quick rub down with a few drops of baby oil on a soft, clean cloth will brighten it up. Rub dry with a towel. This will also remove stains on the chrome trim of kitchen appliances and bathroom fixtures.

▶ Plain white china is very cheap second-hand.

▶ Buy china in 'seconds' shops where designs made for the export market often appear as cut price 'rejects'.

- *Reuse plastic bags; give them to your local small shop who would like them, take them shopping, use them for lining waste paper baskets or pedal bins.*
- *Get your boiler serviced in summer – it's less expensive then and you are not competing for the engineer's time with everyone else who has forgotten to do it earlier.*

Thrifty home decorating and maintenance

Insight

Balance up the cost of cheap paint with the amount of satisfactory coverage it will give you. Sometimes it is worth buying a more expensive product if it will last longer and be easier to apply.

Taking out a loan may be the best and easiest way to raise cash to spend on a home improvement project. If home improvements like an extension or a new kitchen are required then a secured loan is best. Such loans are secured against a property so only homeowners can apply. The thriftiest way to take out a loan is to get a broker to work for you and discuss the options with you.

When decorating and maintaining your home remember:

- *Use water-based rather than oil-based paints and varnishes. You don't need white spirit and the brushes last longer.*
- *Buy trade paints from builders' merchants rather than retail paints. They are cheaper, go further, have good colours and are easier to apply.*
- *Look for discount ceramic tiles. There are always plenty of sources for these and unless you have set your heart on hand-made tiles from Italy they can be as attractive as more expensive ones.*
- *Borrow tools for occasional jobs around the home or hire them for a weekend.*

- *You can make good savings in home supplies from baths to flooring and fabrics by buying in large French hypermarkets. Make sure to check sizes and compatibility when buying fittings.*
- *Use wax crayons to fill small gouges or holes in wooden flooring or furniture. Choose a colour that matches the wood, melt the crayon in the microwave on medium power over a piece of greaseproof paper until you have a pliant piece of wax. Fill the hole using a plastic knife. This can be used to fill quite deep scratches in wooden furniture.*
- *Conceal small scratches or gouges in white, plastic kitchen appliances or the bath with a dab of correction fluid. When it's dry protect the repair with clear nail varnish.*
- *Paint a wall in your baby's room with little animals and birds instead of buying expensive Peter Rabbit wallpaper and friezes. Get your ideas from your child's favourite picture book.*
- *Painting your old floorboards with floor paints – a trompe l'oeil carpet or rug or a diamond pattern – can be effective or simply paint a plain colour and lay a kilim or other rug on top.*

Thrifty ways with workers

- *Get three quotes before deciding which builder to use for any job in the home. Don't necessarily choose the cheapest, just the most realistic.*

Insight

Ask friends and neighbours for information on local work people and keep the contact numbers where you can find them. Recommendations are nearly always better than hopeful contacts through Yellow Pages.

- *Make sure anybody doing any major renovation work is insured. Then, if they are hurt or the job goes wrong or the builder goes bankrupt, you will be protected.*
- *Tell your insurers before any work starts, otherwise they may not allow a claim. If any electrical, gas or plumbing work is*

done, make sure the person doing the work is properly trained and certificated.

▶ *Don't rely on the workforce to buy such equipment as taps and shower heads. It is more satisfying to get yourself a business card and go down to the builders' or plumbers' suppliers yourself where you will get up to 20 per cent off.*

▶ *Pay the builder at agreed stages of the work. He may need some money up front for materials but never pay the whole lot until all the work is done and you are satisfied with it.*

▶ *Avoid using plumbers if you can. To prevent blocked drains, never pour hot fat down the drain and keep a plunger under the sink in case of blockages.*

▶ *Contact your local school to see if any children would be willing to do gardening, odd jobs or car cleaning, for a little pocket money.*

Improvised furniture

How much furniture do you really need? A bed, a table and some chairs should be enough to start off with. As a thrifty expert you won't be buying your furniture on credit so you may have to improvise while waiting to afford what you really want. Folding chairs can be bought very cheaply and will fit well into a small space, they are also portable so can be moved from room to room as necessary. Buying old furniture in junk shops can be fairly expensive if it is masquerading as antique, but if it's just cheap old basic furniture it may be just what you want.

▶ *A cheap pine dresser can be divided up into two pieces and used separately: the top half as a set of shelves, the bottom half as a cupboard.*

▶ *Buy a cheap pine cupboard and stand a set of shelves on top of it, creating a tiny dresser.*

▶ *A couple of trestles with a flush door firmly fixed on top will make a good kitchen or dining table.*

▶ *A decorator's folding table will make an acceptable dining table if covered with a pretty cloth.*

- Recycle a collection of battered old dining chairs by painting them in a bright colour of gloss paint, creating a stunning set.
- Make a single bed by laying a flush door over a timber frame. Drill holes in the door for ventilation and buy a foam mattress. The foam should conform to safety regulations and be at least 12 cm thick.
- Glue five or six aluminium cans together side by side and stick them on the wall to create a sculptural set of storage tubes for items such as pens, pencils, tubes of glue, scissors and balls of string.

Soft furnishings

- Indian cotton bedspreads are cheap and can be used as curtains or throws or cut up and turned into cushion covers.
- If you don't have enough material to cover a complete window, make café curtains that cover only the bottom half of the window. Cotton gingham is cheap, fresh-looking and traditional. Temporary café curtains can be made with crêpe paper tacked, stapled or stuck to the lower half of the window.
- Uncovered cushions stuffed with kapok are available cheaply from department stores. It's the covers that are expensive and you can make those yourself. Old eiderdowns and pillows from jumble sales and charity shops will provide stuffing for new cushions even more cheaply, which you can cover with pieces of fabric left over from curtains or old kilims/rugs.
- Junk shops often have interesting and attractive bedspreads and curtains.

Thrift in the bathroom

- Save about 40 litres of water at a time by having showers instead of baths – but get a high-efficiency shower rather than a power shower. Power showers use as much water as baths.

- *Each flush of the toilet wastes 12 litres of water – but if you put a brick in your cistern you can save up to 3,000 litres a year. Special bricks called save-a-flush or hippos are offered free to customers by many water suppliers. Log on to your supplier's website and see if they provide them. And while you're waiting for yours to arrive use a real brick, which has the same effect.*
- *If you are changing your toilet check out dual-flush toilets which give you the choice of a quick or long flush.*
- *Keep old toothbrushes for cleaning in corners, round taps and scrubbing horrible things from the soles of trainers.*

Insight

I can't get a standard bath mat in my tiny bathroom so I cut it into two and taped up the cut end with carpet tape to stop it fraying. That way I have two bath mats for the price of one – and that fit into the space nicely, too.

- *Add water to the last of shampoos and bath foam bottles to get another two or three uses from them.*
- *Rub a cut lemon over your hands and the scaly bits on your elbows to get a smoother, softer skin.*

Thrifty medicines

- *Most NHS treatment is free in the UK but there are charges for some things such as NHS dental charges, the cost of glasses and contact lenses, travel costs to and from hospital for NHS treatment, travel costs for travelling abroad for treatment, abdominal and spinal support, support tights and wigs. In some cases you may be eligible for help with prescription charges.*
- *If you live in the UK and need frequent prescriptions you may find it cheaper to pay in advance by buying a pre-payment certificate, which lasts for either four or 12 months. Check first whether you are entitled to free prescriptions. It can be difficult to get a refund once you've paid; get information from the NHS Prescription Pricing Authority.*

▶ *The most expensive medicines are not always the best. Generic medicines are just as efficacious as their branded counterparts and will cost you far less. Online pharmaceutical sites often have lists of generic and branded medicines to compare.*

The home office

Every home has an office, whether it's simply a place where you keep your files and pay the bills, or a full-blown working space where you earn your living.

▶ *Tired of junk mail coming through your letter box day after day? Contact the Mailing Preference Services (MPS) which can get your name removed from mailing lists. It can take three months for the junk mail to stop arriving but the service is free (see Taking it further).*
▶ *Cut down the number of telephone calls for free by registering with the Telephone Preference Service (TPS) (see Taking it further).*
▶ *Review all your subscriptions – to associations, groups, magazines and newspapers. How much do you really use them, how often do you actually read the magazines, go to the meetings, benefit from the memberships? Cancel the ones you have not benefited from in the last year.*
▶ *Paper costs money. How many times have you printed something and thrown it away the next day? Send e-cards rather than paper or card ones if you want to save paper – and stamps. If you do print, use both sides of your A4 paper.*
▶ *Buy some of your office stationery in bulk at a discount, either online or by post.*

Lounging in the living room

▶ *Rent your DVDs with neighbours or a group of friends. Pass the disk along before the due date or watch it together.*

- If you have a stock of your own DVDs and CDs take them in for credit at a local entertainment store.
- Instead of telephoning, talk online with a free internet calling service such as Skype or Vonage.
- Buy an exercise DVD instead of joining an expensive fitness club.
- Save money on a visit to a nail salon by inviting some friends round to do each other's nails.

Children

- Use cloth nappies for everyday use and keep disposable nappies for travelling or special occasions.
- Toy libraries offer services to local children, families and carers, based on regular toy loans for a nominal fee. They offer a range of toys, play sessions, information and advice about play and a meeting place for parents.
- Use the children's section of your public library. It's a great way to spend a free morning or afternoon. There are books to read, seats to sit on and often story-reading as well.
- Recycle large cardboard boxes as toys. They make fantastic boats, houses and forts, not to mention storage boxes.
- Keep old clothes, scarves, handbags and shoes in a 'dressing-up' box.
- Use stacking plastic boxes for used and recycled materials such as decorative papers, ribbons and gift tags for wrapping presents or for inventing your own creations.
- An old jug or jar makes a good holder for paint brushes, pencils and pens, rulers and craft knives. Try to keep everything separate so that you can find what you want easily. Many of these items will keep children happy inventing and creating for hours.
- Get chewing gum out of a child's hair by rubbing peanut butter into the gum and working it down the hair.
- Save on hairdressers by cutting your own children's hair using round-ended, hairdresser scissors.

Make your own

▶ *Keep old Christmas and birthday cards to cut up and create new cards of your own.*

▶ *Tissue paper is a stylish and cheap alternative to wrapping paper and good for making flowers.*

▶ *Photographs fill fat albums that people seldom look at. Use them more creatively to make collages, family birthday or Christmas cards – you can even send them away to be turned into jigsaw puzzles – an excellent diversion at large family gatherings.*

▶ *A collection of buttons, large and small can be used to replace lost buttons or to embellish clothes.*

▶ *Keep the decorative parts of old clothes such as lace, buttons, ribbons, largeish pieces of fabric with which you can create doll's clothes, herbal pillows and lavender bags, a patchwork quilt or a summer gilet or a rag rug.*

▶ *Keep ends of rolls of wallpaper which can come in handy as wrapping paper, dolls' house decoration, lining drawers and much else.*

▶ *Keep old matchboxes and when you have enough get the children to glue them together to create a tiny chest of drawers for pins, earrings, buttons etc.*

▶ *Keep a rag bag of fabrics for making anything from patchwork quilts to dolls' clothes or lining baskets. Look in remnants boxes in department stores for short lengths of interesting fabrics, individual balls of wool and any other item the store is trying to get rid of to go into your rag bag.*

Insight

Have you thought of learning to knit? You may find local courses and there are internet clubs and courses to join. You can make a wide range of scarves, hats, and other clothes which make good presents and can be unique to you.

Pets and vets

Don't hanker after a thoroughbred animal. They are expensive to buy and expensive to run. Go to a local dog sanctuary where, if you have to pay at all, the animal will be cheap. It will also be so very glad to have a good home. There is usually an adoption fee but no matter how reasonable this may be a dog is an expensive hobby what with the feeding and veterinary costs and if you are really short on cash maybe you should consider becoming a volunteer dog walker instead. Volunteering costs nothing and you get to spend lots of time with lots of dogs. Cats are less expensive to keep although still require injections, health checks and food. You can get them comparatively cheaply from cat sanctuaries.

▶ *Dogs can very quickly destroy expensive toys. Instead take a plastic water bottle, throw away the screw top and the plastic ring and let your dog chase, retrieve and chew on it. Once the plastic starts to disintegrate drink some more water and make a new toy.*
▶ *Instead of buying expensive games for your cat, put a little fresh or dry catmint in a muslin bag for them to play with.*
▶ *A bit of frayed clothes line is a satisfactorily frugal chasing and pouncing toy for a cat that will last for ages.*
▶ *Probably the cheapest pet to have is a rat. Rats are inexpensive to buy, don't need vaccinations and seldom have to visit the vet. They are sociable, good tempered and you can feed them on lettuce, carrot tops and carrot peelings, oats, sunflower seeds, and other salad vegetables.*

10 THRIFTY TIPS FOR THE HOME

1   Candles last longer if put into the freezer for a couple of hours before you light them.

2   Get yourself a wind-up radio which needs no batteries – good for while you're having a bath or in the garden.

3   Save power when cooking: a tiered steamer allows you to cook a complete meal over one hob; a microwave, tabletop grill or slow cooker is much cheaper than using the oven.

4   Find out if any of your local colleges offer cheap hairdressing, beauty, osteopathy, massage or physio sessions given by students. Sessions with first-year students may be a bit hit and miss but final year students are usually very professional.

5   If you are sent unsolicited goods and an invoice, don't pay! Hang on to the goods. If they are still with you after six months, you can keep them or give them to the local charity shop.

6   Don't let your coins accumulate. Take along just the change you need every time you go round the corner to buy a newspaper or a carton of milk. Then you can't be tempted by anything else.

7   Water your indoor plants with 'grey water' (water previously used for baths or washing up).

8   Barter or share with friends and neighbours. Offer gardening, ironing, childminding, work processing, letter writing or a bit of DIY or anything you are good at for a reciprocal service.

9 *Ask advice at the beauty counters in department stores –*
you will get the advice, perhaps a free make-up session and
probably free samples as well. The skill is in managing not to
buy anything while you are there.

10 *If you are brave, get your teeth seen to by students in a dental*
college. For complicated work you may wait months to be
treated but it is very cheap and very well monitored.

QUICK REVISION TEST

1 *Name five instances when you can use vinegar as a substitute for household cleaning products.*

2 *Name two ways in which you can use flush doors to make cheap furniture.*

3 *Name two uses for crêpe paper.*

4 *How can you save on sending greeting cards?*

5 *How can you entertain young children for free?*

12

Economical transport

In this chapter you will learn:
- *about cheaper cars and fuel*
- *about using a bike*
- *about saving on public transport*.

The thriftiest everyday transport decision would be to give up your car. You can always hire when you need to or join a local car-sharing scheme. Walking, cycling (or perhaps rollerblading) are the cheapest and most ecologically friendly ways of getting around locally. Next best is public transport. In many areas buses, trains and trams are convenient and cheap so use them whenever possible. There are often special deals for children and the elderly or if you book ahead. It's worth seeking these out. Taxis are seldom a thrifty way of travelling but if there are enough of you in the cab, it can be more economical than taking the car.

If you feel you can't give up the car this year, review the situation next year. Meanwhile, if you really have to have a car, there's a wide choice of economical small cars to choose from. People carriers may make sense if you're going to use all the seats and 4 × 4s if you live on a farm or tow a caravan but a smaller car makes more economical sense for just one or two people, especially if you live in town.

Buying a car

BUYING A NEW CAR

All cars give out carbon dioxide. The amount produced is directly related to fuel consumption. New cars in the UK get tested to make sure their exhaust emissions meet European standards, which have been getting more stringent since the 1990s. The newer the car, the better for the environment. One pre-1992 car without a catalytic converter gives out roughly the same toxic emissions as 20 of today's new cars. A new car also gives you the benefit of the latest advances in safety, security, comfort, performance and fuel efficiency but hidden extras can bring nasty surprises and there is always a rapid initial depreciation.

▶ *Aim to keep a new car for at least three years to spread the cost of rapid initial depreciation.*
▶ *Make sure the quoted cost includes insurance and road tax. Watch out for hidden extras such as delivery and number plates.*
▶ *If considering a part exchange, get an idea of your car's value based on its age, condition and mileage.*
▶ *Remember, if you get a good discount on a new car, you can't expect a generous trade-in price for your old car. You might be better to sell the old one separately.*
▶ *Don't be afraid to haggle. Many dealers will have allowed for bargaining when stating a price.*
▶ *Many dealers offer hire purchase as an option. For this you will be expected to pay a deposit of between 10 and 15 per cent of the cost of the car and you won't be able to sell the car until the finance company has been repaid in full.*

BUYING A USED CAR

▶ *A nearly new car (one to two years old) will give you most of the advantages of a new car without the disadvantage of steep depreciation early on.*

- *A five-year-old car may be an even better economy. You won't get the latest features but it won't lose so much in value and it won't cost you so much in the first place. This is particularly good if you drive less than 10,000 miles (16,100 km) a year.*
- *Repair and maintenance bills may be higher and these costs increase the more mileage you do.*
- *Check that the colour matches the description on the registration document. Any changes in shade from panel to panel may indicate accident damage.*

Insight

If you are over 75 don't give up your car if you wish to go on driving. Many car hire firms won't hire to people over 75 which can be a big handicap.

LEASING

You may want to spread the cost of your motoring across the year, avoiding the peaks and troughs of sudden high repair bills. Look at leasing instead. You pay a fixed monthly amount for the car which generally includes servicing and repairs. Watch out for mileage limits on the contract and remember the car is not actually yours.

LIFT-SHARING AND CAR-SHARING

Lift-sharing is a simple idea intended to reduce the number of cars on the road, cut air pollution and could save you money – and stress. The system works pretty much like a dating agency, but rather than finding your ideal partner, it matches you with a potential driver or passenger who is travelling in the same direction or to the same destination; all you pay is a contribution to petrol costs. If you've thought about giving up your car but still feel you need the use of one for specific journeys, then car-sharing could be for you. Car clubs provide their members with access to the 'hire' of a vehicle when they need one. Vehicles are parked in reserved parking spaces, close to homes or workplaces and can be used (and paid for) on an hourly, daily or weekly basis. Car clubs have a role to play in reducing dependence on the car by giving people access to a car for essential journeys without the need to own one.

▶ *In Europe, more than 100,000 people are members of over 100 clubs, and use car-sharing as an everyday part of their transport mix.*
▶ *One car-club car is said on average to replace five private cars; car-club members can apparently reduce their car mileage by half.*
▶ *Car-sharing schemes allow people to share vehicles for some journeys. Check your local council website for organized schemes in your area.*
▶ *Car-sharing lanes are designed for vehicles with more than one occupant and are being introduced in areas that experience high congestion.*

Choosing your car

Insight

Car design is changing to reflect the need to lower fuel emissions and conserve energy. Check carefully what sort of car you want, consult the experts and read the car magazines before making a decision.

ENVIRONMENTALLY FRIENDLY CARS

Cut down your costs by choosing a car that uses less fuel and produces fewer toxic emissions. Other considerations are size and weight. How much your car weighs is an important factor in how much fuel it uses. In fact, weight is more important than engine size. A heavy car uses a lot of fuel to get going and to stop. But a big engine in a small car can be economical.

Obviously from the thrift point of view, a small car with a small engine is going to cost less to buy and less to run than a macho four-wheel drive, especially in a town. Small cars are becoming more common, more fashionable, more reliable and more of a pleasure to drive. If you are a pensioner with a reduced income, low running costs may be a high priority. Low insurance, low road tax and good fuel economy all help to reduce the cost of motoring.

HYBRID CARS

Several car manufacturers offer models, known as hybrids, that combine technologies. A modern hybrid car is driven by electric motors powered by batteries and a petrol engine which provides extra power when required. Hybrids are, on the whole, cleaner than petrol or diesel. Since the petrol engine runs at an optimal speed, it consumes fuel in a more efficient way than traditional petrol engines. Additional power to the battery comes from kinetic energy from the wheels when the car is slowing down. In the UK the government has introduced a rebate on vehicle tax registration on hybrid or small cars and in the USA hybrid cars can attract valuable tax credits.

FOUR-WHEEL DRIVES

If you are truly thrifty you will avoid a four-wheel drive as the family car. Their fuel consumption is around four per cent higher than for a two-wheel drive with the same style body. If you compare a four-wheel drive with the most economical vehicle that can carry the same load, the fuel consumption could be up to 14 per cent higher for the 4 × 4. If you think you have to have a 4 × 4 choose one of the more fuel-efficient models.

MANUAL OR AUTOMATIC

For smooth driving in traffic, it's tempting to opt for an automatic or a car with continuously variable transmission (CVT). These cars are easier to drive as they have no clutch, and they change gear for you. Unfortunately, they also use more fuel. Traditional automatics may use around ten per cent more than manuals whilst cars with CVT use around five per cent more. A new type of car using 'automated manual' transmission, in which hydraulic and electronic systems take care of the clutch and gear change, can offer a fuel consumption saving compared with 'normal' autos and manuals.

▶ *At motorway speeds fuel consumption evens out and there's not much difference between manuals and automatics.*
▶ *Modern semi-automatic features such as button-operated gear change and automatic clutch control help you use less fuel.*
▶ *Petrol vs diesel.*
▶ *The latest diesels are on a par with petrol cars. They are quiet and smooth thanks to developments such as turbo chargers. Even the diesel has been modified so it's not so awkward to fill or smelly if you get it on your hands.*
▶ *On the road diesel engines warm up more quickly from a cold start than petrol which can take around a mile to get up to temperature. Once warm though, a petrol engine is cleaner than diesel, and gives out lower emissions.*
▶ *Both diesel and petrol cars cost about the same to service, but you may find a diesel car needs more oil changes.*

LIQUEFIED PETROLEUM GAS (LPG)

You can buy a new car that runs on LPG or get your petrol car converted. Cars that run on LPG cost more to buy than petrol or diesel ones. However, LPG works out around a third cheaper than petrol and diesel – once you've done enough miles to recoup the extra cost of the car. The higher your annual mileage, the quicker you'll recover the extra outlay.

THRIFTY FUEL TIPS

▶ *Check and compare official fuel consumption data for new and used cars in any Car Buyer's Guide.*
▶ *If you do frequent short journeys where the engine barely warms up, then a diesel could be better.*
▶ *If you spend most of your time stuck in traffic around town, then a petrol car is best.*

- *Maintain an even speed. A slow crawl in traffic will save gallons as opposed to constantly stopping and starting.*
- *Get your tyres checked regularly. Properly inflated tyres avoid premature wear and tear and mileage. Under-inflated tyres can waste five to ten per cent of fuel.*

TAXES AND CHARGES

- *The price of road tax increases with the car's official carbon dioxide emissions, so it pays to get a smaller, more economical car.*
- *Even though they have lower carbon dioxide emissions than petrol cars, diesels are more expensive to tax, because they produce more toxic emissions.*
- *Some cars that use 'alternative' fuels get a 100 per cent discount from the London Congestion Charge Scheme.*

INSURANCE TIPS

It can be tempting to buy the cheapest insurance you can find but cheap deals will have strings attached. You may find the insurance doesn't cover certain things or the policy might pay out less than other companies or you may be charged a big compulsory excess if you have an accident.

- *Motoring organizations have lists of car models that are cheap to insure.*
- *If you take an advanced driving course you could negotiate a cheaper insurance deal.*
- *If you park your car on your drive or in your garage you may get a cheaper premium than if it is parked in the street.*
- *You may get a discount if you belong to a motoring organization such as the Institute of Advance Motorists or the AA.*
- *Avoid speeding penalities or you will pay more in insurance premiums.*
- *Reducing your annual mileage might attract a lower premium.*

THRIFTY WITH CAR COLOUR

▶ *You can even be thrifty about the colour of your car. For example, don't buy a yellow car if you want to do a good deal when you sell it on.*

▶ *A Ferrari in any colour other than red is less desirable; white is fine for delivery vans and police cars, but not exciting enough for a sports car and whereas bright colours suit sports cars, silver or black are usually preferred for executive cars.*

▶ *The Automobile Association says that the top ten favourite colours for a car are, in this order: blue, red, silver, green, white, black, grey, gold, mauve, yellow.*

Biking

If you want to save hundreds of pounds on your travel costs, get a bicycle. Save yourself over £700 ($1,050) on public transport and over £1,000 ($1,500) on car costs every year by switching to cycling. It's easy to assume that the car is the quickest method of travelling. But in rush hour with a scooter, or an electric bike with its assisted power, you will be able to park conveniently and free of charge in the centre of the town, whereas the car will be delayed in traffic and you will have to pay for a parking space.

▶ *Go to a specialist cycle dealer who can advise on the correct bike for your size and offer services/repairs.*

▶ *Ask for a test ride to try the bike out even if you are asked for a small deposit.*

▶ *If two of you want to buy bikes for weekend trips why not buy a tandem? They go faster, are more aerodynamic – and you only have to buy one.*

- One- or two-seat child trailers mean you can bike with young children.
- If you ride a lot at night, dynamo lights are the cheapest.
- Buy a sturdy lock. Bikes are among the most popular things to steal. The more expensive the bike, the more effective the lock should be.
- A folding bike can be a good way of getting to work. There are more than 50 folding bikes to choose from. They are lightweight, comfortable to ride, may be free to take on public transport, can be practically thief proof, don't take up much space and have a high resale value. Some will even fit into a suitcase and take only seconds to fold up.
- The lighter the bike the more you pay.
- Smaller wheels usually give lighter steering and are usually in one size that anybody can ride.
- A small runabout scooter is great for short journeys to work, to the shop or to run errands; they are also cheaper and less dangerous than a powerful motorbike.

Insight

If you ride a bike, please use the cycle lanes, where they exist and don't ride on the pavement unless you are a young child or the road is highly dangerous. The pavement is primarily for pedestrians.

ELECTRIC BIKES

Electric bikes are fitted with a small motor to help the rider when the going gets tough. The idea is not to make a faster, more powerful vehicle, but simply to make hills easier and miles quicker to negotiate. The end product is a fairly conventional bike, but one that lends a hand when required. A recent survey found that the average electric bike user covered 1,200 miles (2,000 km) per annum replacing three car journeys a week. They don't cost much more than conventional bikes, mechanical wear and tear is about the same, and electricity is so cheap as to be largely irrelevant, but there is an extra expense in terms of battery depreciation. Consequently, an electric bike costs more to run. However, electric bike running costs should really be compared with those of a moped, or a car. With cars costing 50–80 pence ($1.20) per mile, an electric bike can save a great deal of money.

▶ *The advantage of an electric bike over a motorbike or scooter is that you don't need a driving licence or road tax. Parking is free. The average electric bike costs around 1.5 pence (2 cents) per mile to run and has a range of about 10–20 miles (15–35 km) per charge. To charge it up, you simply plug in with a standard 3-pin plug to a standard electricity socket.*

▶ *Electric bikes are new technology, and have not been around for long, but so far they seem to have a better resale value than a conventional bike. A typical electric bike costs more to buy but you should get most of that back if you sell the machine on. Legally, electric bikes are treated like ordinary bicycles so there are no registration fees to worry about. You would be wise to insure it though.*

Train travel

There are literally dozens of possibilities for saving on rail fares. Be patient. It can be quite difficult to get the information you need. But booking a month early, or buying family tickets or travelling at particular times of the day can all be worthwhile.

For example, fares for one journey in the UK can vary from over £200 to less than £40, so it obviously pays to do your research and book early. National Rail's website has a special page listing all the special discounted offers (www.nationalrail.co.uk). Certain Virgin and South West Train routes, including Manchester to Edinburgh and London to Southampton, offer 'Megatrain' fares incredibly cheaply if you book early enough.

▶ *In the UK if you are under 26, over 60 or travelling with children you can cut one-third off many ticket prices with a railcard. These are cheap to buy and last for a year. There are three types of railcard covering the UK: Young Person's (and Student's) Railcard; Family Railcard and Senior Railcard. Railcards are not valid for some journeys so check before you travel.*

▶ *Buy train tickets as early as you can (this can mean 12 weeks early but early booking can still be cheaper as late as 6 p.m. the night before you travel so it's worth checking).*

▶ *You'd think that buying a return ticket would be cheaper than buying two singles but many discount deals are only available on one-way fares so it might be cheaper to buy two one-way tickets.*

▶ *Special fares are often available for part of the route. So if you have time to do your research, buying several tickets to make up your route may be cheaper than just buying one all-the-way ticket.*

▶ *Avoid peak times to get better bargains.*

▶ *A USA Rail Pass is available through Amtrak's website (www.amtrak.com) or through Amtrak agencies throughout the world. It is for international visitors only (if you live in the USA or Canada it is not available to you). There are also special deals for students.*

Coach and bus travel

Insight

Although coach travel is less comfortable and slower than train travel, if you want to save money it's usually the way to go. Coaches such as the Oxford Tube run from Victoria or Marble Arch to the centre of Oxford several times an hour from around £10 return.

▶ *Buses and coaches are often the cheapest way to travel but you should always check if there are any special offers on top of the cheap travel offered anyway. National Express coach network in England and Wales and Citylink in Scotland can take you to most places in the UK and offer good value for money. They sometimes have special offers* such as 'go anywhere for £9' when booking at least seven days in advance. They venture abroad as well.

▶ Anyone over 60 living in England is entitled to free off-peak bus travel in the local authority area where they live. Off-peak travel is when you travel after 9.30 a.m. Monday to Friday and all day at weekends. Some also allow travel in the morning rush hour and in some areas passes can also be used on trams, trains or taxis. Some bus passes cover a wider area, such as a county. It can get complicated, but don't let that put you off – be sure to ask before you travel.

▶ In Wales you can use your pass at any time of day.

▶ If you are over 60 you automatically qualify for route sixty fares, allowing you to travel half price on most National Express services.

▶ In Scotland over 60s are entitled to free, local and long-distance bus travel and older and disabled people can use buses at any time of day including the morning rush hour.

▶ You can often save money by combining bus tickets with admission tickets such as inclusive coach and airport-hotel packages as well as theatre, shows and concert deals and tickets to European destinations.

▶ In the USA, bus or coach is by far the cheapest way to travel. Coaches can be luxury or budget. The 'Chinatown bus' is a generic term describing low price bus companies. Buses are particularly good value in the north-east where there is lots of competition.

▶ Greyhound buses travel everywhere in the USA. They offer a variety of passes including the Discovery Pass (valid for 60 days in the USA and Canada). There is also the Ameripass, the International Ameripass and student cards.

10 THRIFTY TRANSPORT TIPS

1 *Manual cars generally use less fuel than automatics. Small cars are cheaper to insure, have lighter controls, good vision and smaller dimensions so are ideal for learners and newly qualified drivers.*

2 *If you are offered a company car, choose carefully to avoid paying over the odds in tax. Get an estimate of the costs for any car on your shortlist.*

3 *If you live in the UK and travel frequently on the continent, an LPG-fuelled car won't be a thrifty buy because it won't be allowed through the Eurotunnel, even if you can prove the tank has been disconnected or emptied. If you're travelling by ferry, check with the operator before you book.*

4 *It is cost-effective to have your car serviced regularly to maintain engine efficiency and cut fuel consumption.*

5 *Remove unnecessary weight from you car such as car racks, heavy items in the boot. An extra 23–45 kg can increase your petrol consumption.*

6 *Keep windows and sunroof closed at high speeds and use the built-in ventilation system for optimum dynamics.*

7 *Stick to 60 mph (100 kph) on the motorway. If you travel at 80–85 mph (128–136 kph) fuel costs can increase by 25 per cent or more.*

8 *Fill up before getting on the motorway to avoid higher pump prices.*

9 *If you like to get a new car regularly, a personal lease plan will give you the convenience of an all-in monthly payment with no extras except for fuel and insurance.*

10 *Reduce the amount you pay in road tax by buying a smaller, more economical car.*

QUICK REVISION TEST

1 *What is a hybrid car?*

2 *Name four ways in which you can reduce your car's fuel consumption.*

3 *What are the advantages of folding bikes?*

4 *What's the cheapest way of getting around in the USA?*

5 *Name three ways you might get a discount on your insurance premium.*

13

Thrifty leisure time and holidays

In this chapter you will learn:
- *about thrifty opportunities locally*
- *about travelling economically*
- *about saving money on family holidays*.

Leisure time at home

Having leisure time on a tight budget can mean staying in a lot because you can't afford to shop or do other things you might enjoy. The trouble is that, especially in winter, staying at home is not particularly thrifty as you have to heat the premises, will be wanting to boil the kettle to make coffee or tea and can find that being at home is in fact quite expensive. There are several answers to this. One is to go out to the library, which is warm, comfortable, interesting, often has chairs to sit in and is, of course, free. Libraries don't only deal in books but also in CDs and DVDs. They usually have a bank of computers that can be used for an hour or so at a time and may well run courses in various computer skills. Some courses are free, including those for literacy and numeracy as well as some e-learning courses.

A brisk walk can take you out of the house and keep you warm. It's a good way of discovering local parks and, indeed, your locality in general. Most parks have a café where you can get a cup of coffee and a biscuit without breaking the bank. Museums and art galleries are usually free and entertaining and also have places where you can get refreshments.

Get yourself an interest. If you don't fancy letting yourself in for a structured course on a subject, why not meet once a week in a friend's home to play whist or mahjong or do some watercolour painting; or just for coffee and gossip? You can meet in a different friend's house each time; everybody brings biscuits or buns or a contribution to lunch and it doesn't have to cost the earth.

Joining a specialist membership association or club can be a thrifty thing to do. For an annual membership subscription you will receive a journal or newsletter with information on events and attractions, opportunities to meet people with similar interests and there may be special offers relating to your interest too. On the other hand, you can save plenty of money by cancelling memberships you don't actually make use of. Cancel any magazines and journals that you don't have time to read as well.

As for going away on holiday, there are many ways you can beat the financial system, from finding cheap hotels to clocking up the air miles. Don't be mean with your research time, compare special deals and book early if you can.

Thrifty ways of learning

Insight

A course, whether short, long, full- or part-time can be a good way of getting out of the house, finding out more about a subject that interests you and meeting people – or all three.

Think of joining a local course. There are literally thousands of courses run by local authorities or privately, including one-day or weekend courses, termly courses or courses leading to a diploma or degree. Subjects covered range from literature and drama to public speaking, all sorts of crafts, languages and computer skills, local history or gardening. Local libraries often run courses in computer skills for a very reasonable cost, or even free. Find out about these from specialist magazines, from the college concerned or through relevant websites.

The Universities of the Third Age (U3As) in the UK are autonomous, self-help, voluntary organizations which encourage and enable older people no longer in full-time paid employment to help each other to share their knowledge, skills, interests and experience. All U3As are members of the Third Age Trust, a registered charity, which is their national support and advisory body. The word 'university' is used in its original sense of people coming together to share and pursue learning in all its forms. You can join these courses for fun, to meet people, to increase your chance of finding work or simply because the subject fascinates you.

FINANCIAL HELP FOR COURSES

You may be able to get financial help towards the costs of learning and perhaps with related costs like travel and childcare. You could be eligible for funding which you don't have to pay back to cover all or part of your course costs. There are various types of funding such as Learner Support Funds which are available in colleges and school sixth forms to help with learning costs. The funds are prioritized for those who face financial hardship. You may be eligible if you also receive other forms of support.

▶ *Grants and bursaries: you could get a grant which you don't have to pay back. Bursaries are similar to grants but are usually linked to certain professions.*
▶ *Career development loans are deferred repayment bank loans that can help you pay for vocational or work-related learning.*
▶ *For a higher education course, you may be eligible for a student loan or other form of financial support.*
▶ *If you already work, your employer may fund your training. You could get help with costs if you are a trade union member.*
▶ *If you receive benefits you may be able do a course without losing any of your benefits.*

▶ *If you belong to a student union find out if your college has a discounted shop and whether you can buy in other local shops such as stationers and bookshops by showing your student card.*

▶ *Borrow books from the library, instead of buying them.*

▶ *Make the most of computer facilities and the library at your college, learning centre, or local library.*

▶ *If you are disabled and your local college can't offer a course to suit your disability-related needs, the Learning and Skills Council (LSC) in the UK should consider funding a place for you at a 'specialist' college. Such colleges are independent, specifically for students with disabilities or learning difficulties and often residential.*

▶ *If the LSC decide that your needs can only be met by going to a specialist residential college, they have a duty to fund you a place there.*

Leisure thrift near home

There are opportunities for being thrifty from day to day but they may not always be obvious.

▶ *Good hairdressers train their staff so you can often get your hair cut very cheaply by a trainee. It may take longer than usual but can be a real bargain.*

▶ *A sign saying 'Any cut at £6' at a barber's means no hair wash, no blow dry, no hair gel and possibly an unattractive cut into the bargain.*

▶ *Professional hair colouring is expensive. Unless you want a very sophisticated look, use the excellent hair colouring shampoos available in chemists. They are easy, cheap, in good colours and last for five to six weeks.*

▶ *Some English Heritage and National Trust properties such as ancient monuments that don't need staffing are free all year round and so are the many coastal walks owned by the National Trust.*

- *You don't have to give up days out because you're being thrifty. City parks are usually free, and so are country parks, especially if you go by public transport or bike rather than use the car park.*
- *If you are visiting attractions that make a charge, try never to pay full price. Tourist information centres, libraries and many museums will have leaflets and local newspaper announcements advertising local events which often include discount vouchers.*
- *Contact your local radio station for free tickets to recordings of TV and radio programmes. The BBC has an organized system called Audience Services. For popular TV shows try to book 12 weeks ahead.*
- *Many historic churches hold free lunchtime concerts of classical music – a pleasure to listen to and away from the temptations of shopping or an extended working lunch.*
- *Libraries sometimes have meet-the-author evenings where you will have an entertaining time and possibly a glass of plonk.*

Insight

Local libraries often have story-telling sessions after school or in the holidays. Why not make use of these? They keep children entertained and parents may enjoy them too or can use the time to browse.

THRIFTY THEATRES AND OTHER ENTERTAINMENTS

Be on the lookout for discounts whenever you think of going out. Very often theatre tickets can be sold at a discount with a pre-theatre or concert dinner or a discounted rail fare. There are several online sites offering theatre tickets for top shows at a discount.

- *Buy half-price (plus VAT) seats for top London shows on the day at TKTS booth in Leicester Square. Don't be fooled by other ticket agencies that try to imitate this.*
- *No time to queue? Phone individual theatres and ask if they have any 'standby discount tickets' on seats not sold.*

- There may be special discounts for groups or schools.
- Cinema tickets cost less in cheaper areas of the country or town, even when the cinema belongs to a national chain.
- Be flexible: Mondays and Tuesdays tend to be low price cinema days. OAPs may get in cheaper on weekend afternoons. Children may get in cheaper on Saturday mornings. Some cinemas have discounts for films starting before 12 noon and some have a cheap night instead. This varies from cinema to cinema so check what's available near you.

Thrifty travel

BY AIR

- If you are not confined to school dates, book late as the holiday season comes to an end. Tour operators are anxious to sell seats on charter flights that are not fully booked.
- Book out of season if you can. The price of a holiday can change by over £200 ($300) between the beginning and end of August.
- Last-minute cheap holiday deals can be misleading about the true cost of the package. Hidden extras such as in-flight meals, tickets issued on departure and fuel supplements can all add to the price.
- Book your flights online as several airlines offer incentives to increase their online bookings. If you travel a lot, the air miles can build up quickly.
- Some large airlines offer visitors to the USA discount tickets under the name 'Visit USA', allowing mostly one-way travel from one US destination to another at very low prices. You must buy these in conjunction with your international ticket – they can't be bought in the USA. Get information well in advance because the conditions attached to them can change.
- On cheap flights take your own packed meals so you won't have to buy the expensive sandwiches offered on the plane.

AIR MILE KNOW-HOW

▶ Use your air miles up before they expire. A few airlines will allow you to cash them in for other things, such as newspaper or magazine subscriptions. It's not the best option, but it's better than letting them go to waste.

▶ If you can't use your air miles within the specified period, give them away. If you don't travel much, or if you can't get away, most airlines will allow you to transfer them to a friend or donate them to the Red Cross which can use them to help staff reach people in need, or carry relief to disaster victims. The Red Cross works with several airlines to allow this.

▶ See if your hotel or car rental will work with your airline to match your cash for miles.

▶ At certain times of year, airlines may offer more air miles than usual.

▶ To cash in your air miles you may need to follow the 331st day rule, which means you must book your flight 331 days in advance, especially during the airline's heavy travel seasons.

▶ You may be able to redeem your air miles to your advantage if you pick a less busy airport. For example, instead of landing in Paris fly to Chartres.

▶ Some online shopping portals offer air miles as a reward for shopping with online vendors. As long as you only buy things you actually need, this is a good way to add to your current air miles.

▶ Some credit cards offer air miles as a bonus for using the card.

BY TRAIN OR COACH

▶ Visitors to the USA can buy a USA Rail Pass, good for 15 or 30 days of unlimited travel on Amtrak and available through travel agents in many countries. With a foreign passport you can also buy passes at some Amtrak offices in the United States itself. Regional rail passes are also available.

▶ Bus or coach is often the most economical form of travel but it can be slow and uncomfortable (although modern coaches are much like planes inside and for long journeys have toilets and in-coach movies). Special rates are often available for senior citizens and students.

▶ For French rail-based holidays check out the French Travel Service which has a range of tours from elegant historic cities to fascinating areas off the beaten track in Provence, Corsica and the Riviera.

▶ Rail Savers offers motorail services to many European destinations from the South of France to Italy, Germany and Croatia.

▶ 'The man in seat 61'(www.seat61.com) is a website offering helpful advice on train travel with links to destinations in the UK, Europe, Africa, Asia, the Middle East, America and Australasia.

▶ A student travel discount card will get you discounts on accommodation, food and transport if you are travelling internationally or nationally. There are several, such as an International Student Identity Card, a Youth Travel Card, a VIP card and a Nomads card which will give you a two-year membership for the price of one.

BY CAR OR SEA

▶ The Eurotunnel is worth investigating for its special offers. For example, there are short breaks from England to France such as two nights for the price of one in a selection of French hotels within three hours' drive of the Eurotunnel terminal for £49 (if you want to come back that's another £49 of course!). There are also five-day breaks which can save up to half the standard fee. Motorcycles are half the price of a car.

▶ Look for search engines that will find the cheapest ferry from England to places on the continent. DFDS Seaways (www.dfdsseaways.co.uk) has a list of destinations for a number of holidays for couples, families, short trips, and long leisurely holidays. For example, Newcastle to Norway for under £50 per person and family packages from £140.

▶ Brittany Ferries (www.brittany-ferries.com) offers trips to a range of destinations in Europe travelling, for example, with pets, in groups or on sports tours.

▶ P&O Ferries (*www.poferries.com*) offers a range of quick trips (for example, Dover to Calais for a supermarket shopping trip) and mini-cruise packages, say from Hull to Zeebrugge.

Thrifty holidaying

▶ Set up a holiday fund and put in it what you can afford each month. This way you won't still be paying for last year's holiday long after your tan has faded.

▶ When you book your holiday the travel company will always try and sell you travel insurance because they make more money from insurance than they do from selling the holiday itself.

▶ If you can't decide what insurance to get, think about how many times a year you are likely to go away. If it is more than twice a year, including your weekend breaks, then you are better off getting an annual policy.

▶ Stick to your budget, pay up front, don't rely on expensive credit cards and don't set off on holiday before you have finished paying for your last trip. You have to pay not just for flights and accommodation but all the expenses of actually holidaying – all of which will probably go on your credit card without the means to pay it off.

▶ There is no law that says you have to go abroad for your holidays. Why not stay at home every second year and discover some of the reasons foreigners visit your own country? You'd be surprised how interesting your local neighbourhood can be if you make proper use of it.

▶ When booking a holiday it often pays to look around on the internet and arrange things for yourself rather than paying for a ready-made package deal.

▶ Hunt out new hotels which may offer introductory rates for a limited period.

▶ Swap your house: home exchanges allow you to holiday anywhere in the world – all you have to do is pay for your

*travel. You have the benefit of knowing that your own house
is being cared for while you are away. You will have the use of
toys, bikes, books, even a car may be part of the deal. Take a
look at agency websites.*

▶ *Look on the internet for bargains in specialist holidays such as
cruising or skiing or simply accommodation worldwide.*

CHEAP BREAKS

▶ *Hilton/Saga breaks for the over-50s provide an excellent way
of exploring the local area or staying near relations without
having to stay with them. Any participating hotel will offer
bed and breakfast for a minimum of two nights and you get
dinner free on the first night – if you stay for three nights you
get two dinners. If only one of you is over 50 you still qualify.*

▶ *Share a villa with friends. One of the advantages of booking a
villa over a hotel is that you usually pay for the villa, and not
per person, so the more the merrier.*

▶ *Hire a camper van and think of exploring places nearby that
you've always meant to visit. You'll be surprised how many
new and interesting destinations are just one tank of fuel away.
Use your local library to discover interesting destinations.*

▶ *If you are British, holidaying in Europe, make sure you have
a European Health Insurance Card that will cover you for
medical costs. It is available through the Department of
Health (www.ehic.org 0845 606 2030).*

▶ *The online site www.couchsurfing.com allows you to search
for individuals who are offering their sofa to travellers.*

FAMILY HOLIDAYS

▶ *Ferret out the free attractions in cities. In New York for
example, you can take a tour with a Big Apple Greeter,
in which a volunteer shows you round a particular
neighbourhood. You can also enjoy free museums such as
the National Museum of the American Indian and the Sony
Wonder Technology Lab; watch outdoor drama free in Central
Park or take a free cruise on the Staten Island ferry. In London*

you can see buskers and other entertainers in Covent Garden; and watch kite-flying on Hampstead Heath or Primrose Hill. In Singapore you can join a free city tour; in Copenhagen take a bike ride; in Melbourne hop on a City Circle tram.

▶ Consider taking a room in a suitehotel. A suite consists of one ensuite bedroom usually equipped with four beds, a sofa bed, kitchen facilities, work space, radio and TV. Such hotels are popular with families. There may be special packages (e.g. if you stay four nights you get one night at half price; seven nights you get one night free) and there are usually a few extra services, such as laundry or babysitting, free.

▶ Several hotels in the Caribbean have extended the age limit at which children can stay free from 12 to 16.

▶ Try youth hostelling with your family. If you're prepared to share a room with your two under-18s, you can get it at a knock-down price with a really cheap three course meal. The cost of family membership would make this worthwhile.

▶ Go camping. There are comfortable thrifty holidays to be had this way on the Mediterranean for two adults and up to four children, that include a ready-erected tent, proper beds, a fridge, a four-burner stove and activities and fun for all ages.

▶ The larger your family the more thrifty it will be to take your own car to the continent by ferry than to fly and rent a car when you get to your destination. You can sail from the UK to Spain, Scandinavia, Germany, Holland and Belgium. Visit sailanddrive.com for details.

TIPS FOR VISITING DISNEYLAND AND OTHER THEME PARKS

▶ Go prepared with camera film, nappies, sunscreen and other necessities bought outside the park.

▶ If your on-site hotel offers a deal where you buy a souvenir mug the first day and you get free refills at your resort during the length of your stay – grab it. On-site drinks are anything but frugal so you can save a lot.

▶ Don't impulse-buy themed souvenir purchases until you are about to leave by which time you will have an idea which one your child really wants.

- *Avoid a 'character breakfast' which can be dear and concentrate on ways to meet the characters informally as you wander round the park.*
- *Restaurant servings are very large so consider letting two children share one helping.*
- *Look for theme park restaurants that offer deals where children eat free.*
- *Avoid eating a full meal in the classier restaurants. Enjoy the experience by booking a 3 p.m. seating and just have a dessert.*
- *If you plan to visit several parks on your visit, buying a pass which will take in all the parks will be cheaper than buying passes for each park separately.*

WORKING HOLIDAYS

Volunteering your services in some form is a rewarding and thrifty, if not particularly restful, form of holiday. There are a number of organizations arranging holidays from helping to dig wells in developing countries to conserving the countryside.

In the UK the National Trust runs around 450 working holidays every year in England, Wales and Northern Ireland, from carrying out a conservation survey and herding goats to painting a lighthouse or planting trees. Singles and couples from 16 upwards from all walks of life and from all over the world go on National Trust working holidays. They are not free, you pay for your hard work, but not nearly as much as you would for most holidays. No previous experience is necessary – you just need to be team-spirited, enjoy being outdoors in beautiful locations and not mind paying to get your hands dirty.

HOUSE- AND PET-SITTING

Stay in other people's homes and care for their pets and possessions while the owners are away. Although for much of the time you are free to come and go as you please, you take on various responsibilities for the owner. You live in the client's home (which maintains security). You keep the areas of the house that you use clean and tidy; take telephone messages; deal with callers; water houseplants and provide light garden care. If you are happy to home-sit with pets or livestock, you care for them as instructed, maintaining their normal routines.

Insight

If you don't want to spend time in other people's homes, you like animals why not become a dog walker? You can earn a little pocket money and get some outdoor exercise – it's more interesting than jogging.

HOLIDAY OFFERS TO BE WARY OF

▶ *Don't fall for bogus holiday clubs or timeshares. The more you feel bullied by the selling technique, the less interested you should be. Check that dates and destinations are guaranteed. Holidays are often not available when and where you want them; the advertised discounts are often not guaranteed; the resale value may be zero; there may be annual subscription charges to pay whether you use it or not; the company may not be held accountable for any spoken promises made by their sales reps. Never go to a six-hour presentation about a holiday club.*

▶ *If you book a last-minute, cheap holiday deal, don't be misled about the true cost of the package. Hidden extras such as in-flight meals, tickets issued on departure and fuel supplements can all drive the price up.*

▶ *Be wary of any 'free holiday' offers by phone or thrust into your hand while you are abroad. You may have to pay for flights and other add-ons that make it more expensive than if you had booked it yourself. You may also have to go somewhere you don't want to go at a time that isn't convenient.*

Insight

If you are planning a holiday with several people or family groups, check how many individuals are allowed to stay. Some holiday lets specify numbers and may keep a sharp eye on how many people are actually sleeping in the place.

10 THRIFTY LEISURE AND HOLIDAY TIPS

1 *Learn something on a course. There are dozens of subjects to study either just for the interest and companionship or to give you a skill you can use later.*

2 *Find out what concessions there are on public transport in the city of your choice. For example, the Oyster card in London and the Metrocard in New York give you cheaper travel on buses and underground trains; the Paris Pass gives you cheap travel round the city and also free entry to over 60 of the best tourist attractions but also gives you queue-jumping rights at the busiest attractions plus other deals and freebies.*

3 *When going to the cinema make your popcorn at home and bring it with you. Supermarkets sell microwave popcorn bags at around four bags for the price of one bought in a cinema.*

4 *Take your dog, cat or ferret with you on holiday instead of sending it to expensive kennels. The microchip scheme will allow you to do this. But contact your vet in plenty of time as it must be treated not less than 24 hours and not more than 48 hours before being checked-in with an approved transport company for its journey.*

5 *Make the most of air miles. Thrifty planning can enable you to fit in the occasional extra long-haul flight practically free.*

6 *Pay for holidays with cash you have in the bank rather than a credit card. This helps limit your spending and means you can better afford your next holiday.*

7 *Go camping. Modern campsites often have ready-erected tents and all mod cons.*

8 *Get your hair cut by a trainee hairdresser at a well-known salon.*

9 *Use the online search engines to look for cheap deals and discounts at theatres, on ferries, in the air and when hiring a car.*

10 *Take home any item going for the asking such as free mini soaps, mini jams, individual salt, pepper, mustard and sauce packs, paper napkins, airline socks etc.*

QUICK REVISION TEST

1 *In what ways is your local library a thrifty place to spend time in?*

2 *What free entertainments can you look for near your home?*

3 *Name three ways of getting more air miles.*

4 *Name three ideas for saving on family holidays.*

5 *Name five free attractions in capital cities around the world.*

14

Make the most of the garden

In this chapter you will learn:
- *about composting and recycling*
- *how to save water*
- *how to get cheap plants and grow your own food.*

Growing your own garden produce is a thrifty occupation which can save a fair amount in the weekly food bill. Any space out of doors where you can grow things qualifies as a garden, whether it runs to six acres or is just a small balcony. You don't need much space to grow a surprising number of edible plants from culinary herbs to tomatoes, vegetables and, in a sheltered spot, even expensive fruits such as figs and peaches, particularly if you get plenty of sun. You can save substantially if you grow herbs that are expensive to buy such as coriander and basil, and if you grow different types of salad vegetables which are also expensive if bought already washed and bagged. For those with time, an allotment is an inexpensive way of providing an all-absorbing interest, a way of keeping warm and fit in winter and plenty of fruit and vegetables for a whole family.

If growing your own can save you money, your actual gardening can be thrifty as well by finding cheap or free tools and making the ones you have last by maintaining them well. You can also scrounge cheap materials, plants and seeds and recycle as much waste as you can into the garden and compost heap. Composting is thrifty in two ways: it uses up all sorts of household waste that would otherwise have to be bagged up and thrown away and it saves on the costs of buying compost and mulch.

Composting

Home-made compost is a valuable way of improving the soil in your garden without buying expensive bags of commercial compost in the local garden centre. About a third of the average household refuse bin is made up of waste that could be composted, creating a rich source of plant food, organic matter to improve all types of soil, and a mulch to keep down weeds and retain water. There's much rubbish talked about composting and a strange mystique retained about how it should be done, but in fact, it's not difficult and it's free.

▶ *Ask your local authority if they supply subsidized home compost bins.*
▶ *Better still, build your own 1 m × 1 m (3 ft × 3 ft) compost bin using wooden slats. Cover with an old carpet. Having two bins means you can fill one while the other is rotting down.*
▶ *Composting is the best way of recycling green waste and much better than putting it out to be collected for landfill. Fill your bin loosely with a mixture of ingredients so that it has plenty of air.*
▶ *Put in a good mixture of different types of waste; add crumpled newspaper and cut up cardboard if it all gets compressed and airless. If this does happen you are probably trying to cram too much into the bin and compressing it down.*
▶ *Water the compost if it gets very dry in hot weather.*
▶ *Be patient. It will rot down in time whatever you do. If you have two bins, fill one up, allow a year for it to rot while you fill up the second.*

WHAT YOU CAN COMPOST

> **Insight**
>
> The important thing about composting is to mix up the different ingredients in thin layers of compostable materials – not one great tipping-in of grass cuttings followed by two buckets of vegetable peelings. And don't cram the compost down: it needs air.

▶ *Fruit skins, vegetable peelings, tea bags, coffee grounds, crushed eggshells.*

▶ *Grass cuttings – not all together but in layers with the other ingredients.*

▶ *Hedge clippings, old plants and flowers.*

▶ *Crumpled or shredded card and waste paper including cardboard tubes and egg boxes (not plastic ones).*

▶ *Wood ash, but not coal ash.*

▶ *Human hair and animal fur.*

▶ *Old wool, cotton and linen clothes.*

▶ *Chopped straw, hay and bedding from vegetarian pets such as rabbits.*

WHAT YOU CAN'T COMPOST

▶ *Cooked food, meat and fish.*

▶ *Dairy products.*

▶ *Droppings from meat-eating animals.*

▶ *Magazines and heavily inked cardboard.*

▶ *Nappies.*

▶ *Coloured or shiny paper.*

▶ *Coal ash and soot.*

▶ *Plants infected with persistent diseases such as clubroot, white rot or blight.*

▶ *The roots of persistent weeds such as bindweed or couch grass.*

▶ *Synthetic fabrics.*

▶ *Glass, plastic or metal which should all be recycled separately.*

COMPOSTING MEAT AND COOKED FOOD

Most composting systems are not suitable for meat and cooked food products. However, there are special domestic composters available to enable you to turn all your kitchen waste into a nutritious soil-improving compost in just a few weeks. A Green Cone or a Green Johanna also allow you to compost all your food products. These systems use a combination of solar energy, oxygen and natural bacteria which digest all food waste created by the average household, including all cooked and uncooked meat, bones, fish, dairy products, bread, pasta, vegetables and fruit into either their natural components of water and carbon dioxide with a minimal residue (Green Cone) or when garden waste is added, into a rich compost (Green Johanna). Both products are made using recycled materials.

ALTERNATIVES TO TRADITIONAL PRODUCTS

▶ *For a quick, easy, cheap and safe weedkiller, mix 30 ml (1 fl oz) vodka, a few drops of washing up liquid and 400 ml (14 fl oz) water in a spray bottle. Apply in full sunshine to weeds growing in direct sunlight. It won't work in the shade. The alcohol breaks down the waxy covering on the leaves, making them susceptible to dehydration.*
▶ *WD40 sprayed directly onto bee or wasp stings is said to soothe the pain immediately.*
▶ *Chop up banana skins and place or bury them under rose bushes as a nutrient.*
▶ *Tomato fertilizer is cheaper than specialist fertilizers for different plants (such as roses, clematis and fruit and vegetables) and will benefit all.*

- *Your own garden-made compost is an excellent mulch and fertilizer.*
- *Make your own free fertilizer from weeds. This one is good for an allotment rather than for a small garden: fill a large lidded container with weeds – leaves, roots and all. Include nettles and comfrey if you have them. Fill the container with water and cover it tightly with the lid because as it ferments it smells disgusting. A few weeks later put on a mask and gloves and transfer a ladleful of this mixture into a watering can. Dilute with clean water until it is a pale brown colour and feed it to your plants. This saves on the tomato fertilizer. When it's all used up tip the dregs onto your compost heap.*
- *Make a liquid fertilizer by putting a (gloved) handful of fresh nettles into a pan, cover with 600 ml (1 pt) water and bring just to the boil. Remove the pan from the heat; allow it to cool while still covered. Strain the liquid and dilute with four parts of water. Add a dessertspoon of washing up liquid which helps it to adhere to plant foliage and spray as soon as possible as a foliar feed. This is also effective against mildew, blackfly and greenfly.*

COMPANION PLANTING

Some plants seem to be good for other plants in a variety of ways so companion planting can reduce the need for pesticides and fertilizers because when grown near other plants they will keep pests away or encourage healthy growth.

- *French or African marigolds (Tagetes) are effective grown amongst tomatoes and potatoes to protect them from pests such as whitefly. Both the smell and excretions from the roots deter the fly.*
- *Grow foxgloves near apples to encourage disease resistance.*
- *Sage, mint, thyme and rosemary are all beneficial to cabbages.*
- *Borage is good for strawberries.*
- *Plant a clove of garlic beside each rose in your garden to protect it from greenfly.*

Insight

Remember that you can recycle quite a lot into the compost heap including torn-up paper bags, old cardboard boxes, and use old shoe boxes to file seed packets, growing instructions, postcards and other paraphernalia.

Use your ingenuity to find ways of recycling both garden tools and other objects in the garden. Here are a few ideas to point the way:

▶ *Remove the fabric from an old umbrella and use it as a support for a low-growing rose or clematis, a cucumber or courgette plant.*

▶ *Use plastic knives with permanent marker as plant labels.*

▶ *Use nylon knee-highs to tie young trees and shrubs to their supports.*

▶ *Use old tights to protect delicate fruit such as peaches from the ravages of birds or squirrels. They do look strange but are effective.*

▶ *Use crushed soft drink cans in the bottoms of containers to help drainage.*

▶ *Handles of broken hoes and rakes make excellent sturdy supports for newly planted trees and shrubs.*

▶ *Blend together equal amounts of live-culture yoghurt and water with a handful of moss. Use a paintbrush to spread the mixture in a cool, shady spot where you want moss to grow, for example, between the cracks in paving or up the sides of flowerpots. Keep misting the moss with water until it is established.*

▶ *Recycle old carpet off-cuts by laying them in the vegetable garden over winter to keep the weeds down. You can also use them as a sort of 'breathing lid' to conserve heat and retain moisture on a home-made compost heap. Any old carpet will do to keep weeds down but on the compost heap use only natural fibres so they can eventually rot down and become part of the compost.*

▶ *Damaged compact discs make good bird scarers.*

▶ *If you have to support a large old tree, nail the sole of an old shoe or trainer to a stout post to protect the tree branch from the hard edges of the post.*

Frugal containers

Plant pots and containers can be very expensive if you buy them new. Avoid garden centres and home stores if you don't want to be seduced by antique pots imported from the Mediterranean or brightly glazed pots from China and think laterally. You can plant in almost anything that will hold compost and you probably have a host of suitable containers already lying around in the house or garden.

▶ *If you are concentrating on vegetables and don't mind a utilitarian look, start off with metal or plastic buckets. They don't last forever in the house so when they become damaged punch a few holes in the bottom or sides and use them for tomato, aubergine or pepper plants.*

▶ *On the patio you may want more attractive containers for things like pelargoniums and busy lizzies, such as an old kettle, second-hand mixing bowls, enamel jugs and saucepans. Charity shops, junk shops, jumble sales and car boot sales are all likely sources for suitable containers.*

▶ *Make your own seed pots out of rolled up newspapers which biodegrade easily and minimize root disturbance when planting out.*

▶ *Black buckets retain heat which is good for northern gardens.*

▶ *Old car or lorry tyres can contain herbs that spread, such as mint, or be stacked up to hold rhubarb plants. If you don't like them black, paint them more cheerful colours with paints left over from home decorating.*

▶ *A roll of wire netting can make a large container for potatoes. Half fill with compost, plant the potatoes and earth them up as their leaves grow – they don't mind being covered and will simply grow higher. You can remove the netting to harvest the potatoes.*

▶ *Make your own grow bags from sturdy bin liners filled with home-made compost mixed with garden soil and pet bedding or well-rotted horse manure or chicken litter to add nutrition. Tape up the end and cut holes for the plants.*

- *Grow tomatoes and peppers on the patio in a black bin liner hidden in an attractive basket.*
- *Old bicycle tyres and inner tubes make strong but flexible tree ties and gate hinges.*

Cheap seeds and plants

BARGAIN PLANTS

Plants and even seeds can be expensive, especially when you are stocking up a garden from scratch. Nurseries are obviously not into giving away their plants but occasionally they may be almost out of a particular variety and the last specimen is a pathetic one. In this case you could ask how much they will reduce the price because of its sickly condition. Friends and neighbours will often have redundant roots when replanting in the autumn. You could probably swap for something you have that they would like. Any herbaceous plant that dies down in the autumn is satisfactory for this sort of treatment. Bulbs too can be thinned and passed on. Use your thrifty ingenuity to get plants free or for almost nothing:

- *Landscape gardeners or people maintaining public parks can be approached while they are clearing or planting during spring and autumn. They nearly always have plants left over which they may be willing to let you take. You have to be around on the right days when the work is being done. If you are hopeful, take some big plastic bags and a fork with you.*
- *Gardens open to the public often sell small pots of the plant varieties they grow in the garden and that can be a cheap way of obtaining interesting and unusual plants at good prices.*
- *Occasional plant sales can be a rich source of cheap plants. Sometimes local specialist nurseries may get together to sell, otherwise specialist organizations such as the Hardy Plant Society or the Cottage Garden Society in the UK may have a plant sale on the day of their AGM. Such sales are often*

advertised in the local paper and if you are a member of the
society, the newsletter will let you know of opportunities.

▶ Shop in your local garden centre at the end of the season
when they are trying to clear out ready for the next season.

▶ Specialist nursery gardens, where plants are propagated, are
often cheaper than garden centres. If you visit in mornings
and non-busy times you can often cultivate a relationship
with the owner which might produce discounts.

▶ Wholesale nurseries which sell to the trade are a good source
of cheap plants, including vegetable and salad seedlings and
bedding plants in trays, provided you are prepared to buy
enough plants. Perhaps you could share them with friends?

▶ Collect your own seed – from non-hybrid plants. Wait until
the seeds are ripe, allow them to dry out and store them in
labelled envelopes. Some societies have a free seed collection
and distribution service, which is well worth taking part in.

Insight

Some seeds need special treatment before they will sprout.
Get a book, check with your local garden centre or online
garden advice site to find out whether your seeds should be
dried, frozen, scraped or prepared in some other way relevant
to their particular needs.

▶ Collect your own cuttings from your own or friends' gardens –
with permission and NOT from gardens open to the public or
botanic gardens. Shrubs and shrubby plants will usually take
easily. To make cuttings, remove healthy, pest- and disease-
free shoots about ten centimetres long. Trim off the lower
leaves and cut cleanly beneath a leaf joint. Insert in compost
in a small pot. Water and don't forget to label.

▶ Join your local garden club or community garden group,
where you will rub shoulders with others with similar
interests. This is a good way to enter into plant swapping,
discuss gardening experiences and problems, and perhaps
get discounts on tools and products.

▶ Keep your eyes open in your own garden for interesting plants
that have sown themselves. You can then pot them up and when
they are big enough replant them where you actually want them.

- ▶ *Scoop seeds out of tomatoes, cucumbers or courgettes onto pieces of kitchen paper and let the jelly dry out. Put them in an envelope and plant them in spring.*
- ▶ *Seeds don't always expire by the date printed on the pack. Pre-soak old seeds in a little water to help them on. It won't work with all seeds but is always worth a try.*
- ▶ *Start your seeds in cardboard egg cartons which will eventually disintegrate when you plant them, or in the bottoms of eggshells.*
- ▶ *Use an inexpensive fluorescent tube instead of an expensive grow-light to start seedlings.*

Saving water

Water bills keep rising and the garden is an obvious water guzzler, so it makes frugal sense to find ways of using less water. It is estimated that lawn and garden watering can take up at least 40 per cent of total household water use. There are two things you can do; one is to water much less in the garden, growing only plants that can cope with your particular garden conditions without too much nannying. The other is to collect rainwater in water butts filled from the down pipe of your home's gutters. Rain on an average-sized roof should produce about 2,400 litres of water a year. Inexpensive plastic water butts are available in garden centres but you may be able to get one more cheaply or even free through your local authority. Two water butts would be better than one – they can be joined by a flexible hose so that when one is full it feeds into the other, then when there is a drought you are well-prepared.

Insight

In general, once a plant has settled in, don't water it, even in a drought. Many plants will put down roots to reach water deep in the soil and can manage OK, whereas if you water them their roots will try to get nearer to the surface and come to rely on your watering.

If you happen to be digging up the garden for any reason, why not take the opportunity to bury a large tank in the garden. The water collected can be pumped up quite cheaply and can provide not only water for the garden but for indoors as well. Meanwhile heed the following watering tips:

▶ *Water pots and containers early in the morning or late at night when the sun won't dry them out so quickly.*
▶ *Water the roots rather than the leaves.*
▶ *Use plastic bottles as a cheap way of irrigating plants rather than buying watering kits from garden centres. Cut a hole in the bottom, remove the cap and bury the bottle, with just the cut edge showing, near the roots of plants that need watering. Fill up with water when necessary. This waters just the roots and isn't wasted on the surrounding soil.*
▶ *Grow plants that will survive without much watering. (But remember, when putting in any new plant you will need to keep it watered for several months until it is established.)*
▶ *A soaker hose system can be run above ground or buried near the plants that need water most and can water the roots of plants round the entire garden comparatively economically.*
▶ *Mulch round your established plants to prevent the soil from drying out so quickly. You can mulch with straw, leaf mould, compost, dried bark or even gravel.*
▶ *Add water-retaining hydrogels to your potting compost. They hold several hundred times their weight in water and release it gradually to the plants' roots.*

LAWN-WATERING TIPS

▶ *If you must water your lawn, give it a good sprinkling once a week rather than a half-hearted sprinkling every day and don't let any water be wasted on paths or a drive. The soil should be saturated to about five centimetres/two inches.*
▶ *Allow your lawn to lie dormant. Lawn grasses are adapted to summer drought, and, although they may turn brown, will green up when the rain comes again.*

▶ *Cut down on mowing during a drought. Raise the mowing height, allowing the slight shade from the taller grass to reduce water loss.*

▶ *Mow during the coolest part of the day and leave the grass clippings which return small but valuable amounts of moisture to your lawn.*

Grow your own

Growing your own vegetables, fruit and herbs can save a substantial amount in fresh food supplies. It can be frustrating if you have foxes, deer, rabbits or squirrels to contend with but even they give opportunities for thrifty thinking in the ways you can devise to deter and balk them. The thriftiest way to garden is 'organically', that is to say to create a garden whose soil is rich and full of living organisms, which provide nutrients, and which consists of a wide variety of plants, including trees and shrubs to encourage wildlife which will help to keep pests under control. This sort of garden requires practically no chemical products and modern gardening techniques make it quite easy to do.

Concentrate on producing good, well-aerated soil full of tiny micro-organisms and worms for your garden rather than relying on expensive chemical treatments. A healthy soil already has all the ingredients required to produce healthy plants which can fight off pests and diseases. A diverse garden encourages wildlife of all kinds which will help to keep pests under control.

Insight

Containers for vegetables can be on a patio where you can keep an eye on them and protect them from pests such as slugs and snails. Suitable vegetables include runner beans (grown up a pyramid frame), tomatoes, potatoes, peppers and aubergines, ruby chard, spring onions and squash (round an arch).

THRIFTY BY ALLOTMENT

An allotment is a great money-saver and a great way of acquiring a garden if you do not have one attached to your home. All you need to begin with is time, energy and seeds or seedlings. You can then enjoy eating your produce throughout the year and, if you grow a vine, even make your own wine. There may be a waiting list, so it's often worth ringing the allotment organizers at regular intervals to let them know you are still interested. You might be able share a plot while waiting for an allotment to become free.

WHAT TO GROW

▶ *Many herbs are a delight to grow, unfussy, sweetly scented, disease- and pest-free and long-flowering. Try chives, marjoram, thyme, rosemary, sage and mint.*
▶ *If taking on a disused allotment, put it all down to potatoes or comfrey for the first year to clear the ground. There are lots of unusual potatoes to try and comfrey is excellent for the compost heap.*
▶ *Easy and rewarding are marrows, courgettes, leeks, everlasting spinach, purple sprouting broccoli, radishes and several types of lettuce.*

USING YOUR WEEDS

▶ *Ground elder (Aegopodium podagraria) is the gardener's scourge because it's almost impossible to get rid of – so eat it as a vegetable. Wash the leaves and cook them as you would spinach.*
▶ *The stinging nettle (Urtica dioica) has dozens of uses: the cut leaves and stems are excellent on the compost heap and can be made into a good liquid fertilizer (see p. 229).*
▶ *Nettles can also be used to make a nourishing soup or turned into wine or beer.*

10 THRIFTY GARDENING TIPS

1 *Fill a large bucket with sand and pour in about one litre of clean motor oil. Store, clean and lubricate garden tools such as hoes, rakes, spades and forks by plunging them in the sand.*

2 *A straight ladder or front part of a stepladder makes a shallow planter with ready-made sections that look appealing filled with annuals, herbs or salad greens. The annuals can be used as cut flowers and the herbs and salads for delicious meals.*

3 *Put your garden string in a small metal teapot with the end of the string coming out through the spout. The string will be easier to find and easy to unravel.*

4 *Use wire coat hangers to pin down stems of plants when taking stem cuttings. They can also be bent into practically invisible plant supports.*

5 *Join a national gardening organization such as the Royal Horticultural Society or a local gardening association or club. Many meet regularly for lectures, arrange plant sales, garden visits and organize discounts on garden products.*

6 *Slug killers are expensive and often dangerous to wildlife or pets. A cheap answer is to cut a grapefruit in half and put the shells upside down near the favourite plants of slugs or snails. In the morning, collect up the slugs that have collected underneath and replace the shells. When they begin to go mouldy, put them on the compost heap.*

7 *Acid-loving plants such as camellias, azaleas, rhododendrons and magnolias appreciate used coffee grounds so put them around the base of the plant where the roots can benefit.*

8 *Use your compost heap to unburden yourself of fruit skins, vegetable peelings, tea bags, coffee grounds, crushed eggshells, grass cuttings, hedge clippings, prunings, old plants and*

flowers, crumpled or shredded card and waste paper, wood ash, hair and fur, wool and cotton throw-outs, chopped straw, hay and bedding from vegetarian pets.

9 Get free plants in spring or autumn from the replanting in local parks or swap plants with friends.

10 Water plant containers early in the morning or late at night when the sun won't dry them out so quickly.

QUICK REVISION TEST

1 *Name five things you should not put on the compost heap.*

2 *How can you use old carpets and rugs in the garden?*

3 *Name five ways of saving water in the garden.*

4 *How can nettles help the garden?*

5 *How can you use bicycle tyres and inner tubes?*

15

Earn a little something

In this chapter you will learn:
- *about selling things from your home*
- *how to make the most of your skills*
- *how to make the most of holiday jobs*.

There are all sorts of ways in which you can earn a small addition to your income. You can, for example, sell objects languishing in your attic at the occasional car boot sale, take on manual work in the summer holidays, walk somebody else's dogs or sell items on eBay.

Tax implications

If you do decide to make a little extra, find out whether you have to pay tax on the extra that you make. Contact your tax advisor or your local tax office to ask advice before you start earning to find out when any earnings will become liable for tax and to make sure that it won't push you into a higher tax bracket. If you trade on eBay for example, you should register your trading activities within three months of starting to trade or face a hefty penalty and interest on unpaid tax. The rules apply to all sole traders, whether they use the internet or not but bear in mind that because of the explosion in popularity of online auction sites, the tax men monitor such sites with eagle eyes. It is not thrifty to try and get the better of the tax man. People making the odd trade online to get rid of unwanted gifts or personal possessions are not considered traders but anyone who is specifically buying goods to sell for profit is considered to be trading.

If you are trading online or in any other way such as at a market stall or car boot sale, you should become familiar with the legal implications of doing so. If you attend car boot sales on a regular basis, even if it is only once every two months, for example, you may be regarded as a trader and if you employ anyone and/or sell the same type of goods from other venues such as markets or from home, you will almost certainly be a trader in the eyes of the law. You should then understand the law with regard to such things through the Business Names Act, the Consumer Protection Act, the Fair Trading Act, the Price Marking Order and the Food Safety Act.

If you are registered with a benefits agency you should let the agency know whether you are earning or even if you are just doing voluntary work.

Work from home

Don't be taken in by work-at-home advertisements that promise a large income for minimal work such as envelope-stuffing, craft assembly work or any other jobs. They offer quick cash, minimal work, and no risk with the advantage of working when it's convenient to you. What they don't tell you is that you might have to work many hours without pay or pay hidden costs to place newspaper ads of your own, make photocopies or buy supplies, software or equipment to do the job. Legitimate work-at-home business promoters should tell you in writing exactly what is involved. Before you become committed find out what your tasks will be; whether you will be paid a salary or work on commission; who will pay you; when you will get your first payment; the total cost of the programme including supplies, equipment and membership fees; and ask if you can speak to somebody already working for the company.

HOME, CHILD AND PET-SITTING

When people leave their home, whether for the day, a week or a month, it is soothing for them to know there is someone responsible and reliable to care for the place and its inhabitants. Caring for other people's homes can be turned into an almost full-time occupation or be part-time and as regular or irregular as you like. But you will often be competing against a whole lot of other applicants for such jobs. House-sitting is a good occupation for retired people and babysitting can be good for the young. If you are in the middle of relocating, house-sitting might fill the hiatus. House-sitting offers comfort and variety but you probably won't make much money so won't be saving up for a home of your own. You can either house-sit as an occasional holiday job or make it a more or less permanent way of life with a caravan or houseboat permanently parked somewhere for the odd weeks between jobs.

Since many house-owners will have pets for you to look after as well, make sure everything is written down for you from care of the home to care of the pet and where to get hold of the plumber in case of need. If you go through an agency there will be a number of requirements. For example, some agencies require that, apart from loving dogs or cats, you must have a computer with an internet connection and a working printer; a working mobile phone; be prepared to go for walks in all weathers; and be willing to sign a six-month contract. There are many websites advertising house-sitting jobs. Most charge a fee for being on their books. Check on the agency through a house-sitter discussion forum before you send any money.

If you are new to house-sitting consider taking jobs free until you build up a few references. After all, you are getting bed and board in a comfortable home. But there may be extra tasks involved such as pet care or garden maintenance. In this case the job can be seen as a service and a small fee can be involved.

At a simpler level, you can simply become a dog walker or be prepared to pop in regularly to feed someone's cats and give them quality grooming. Obviously you should enjoy animals and have experience with them. Large dogs or packs of dogs will need somebody energetic and strong. Word of mouth is a valuable form of advertising. When you have acquired expertise and confidence in dealing with other people's pets, put up a notice in your local vet's surgery, advertise in the local paper or go through an agency. Many agencies exist to match pet-owners to pet-minders. Begin by taking care of the dogs of neighbours, friends or relatives.

Babysitting jobs are always available for people who are qualified to fill them. It's a good way for sixth formers or college students to earn a little cash. But although it sounds easy, you can be a mediocre or good babysitter. If you get a certificate in cardiopulmonary resuscitation (CPR) it will reassure parents that you can cope with emergency situations. Contact your local Red Cross or the health or fire department to learn about CPR certification classes in your area. Why not find out if babysitting classes are held through your local authority. As with pet-sitting, it's a good idea to begin with a family you know, where you know the baby and its ways. Make sure you feel sure of the family who hires you and that both parties are clear about any rules and expectations.

Insight

Schoolchildren can start by looking after friends' babies for short periods until they prove themselves to be reliable and responsible. It's a good way for them to learn to care for others.

CAR BOOT SALES AND GARAGE SALES

De-cluttering the home is a great way to make room and give a new look to the place. But don't just throw everything away. Take your junk to car boot sales and get a little extra cash. (Jumble sales are different – they are held for a purpose – to make money for a particular charity so you donate everything you offer and don't expect any money back.) Things always sell better if they look good so clean up old tables, paint chairs, polish up bits of old brass but don't expect huge profits. Old videos and CDs are popular and so are books and toys. You can even sell plants. The whole point about car boot sales is that people go to find bargains so you can't expect to make much money – but it can be a fun day out and satisfying to go home with even a little cash for small luxuries and more space in your home.

- ▶ *Don't put price labels on your goods and be prepared to bargain. You will be better able to price objects when you see what other people's items are selling for.*
- ▶ *One advantage of car boot sales is that buyers pay cash and take their purchases away themselves.*
- ▶ *Pack items in small cardboard boxes or carrier bags which makes them easier to carry than if you stuff them into a huge suitcase.*
- ▶ *Take a wallpaper table or trestle table for your goods and a folding stool to sit on.*
- ▶ *Arrive early. You want to be able to unpack before the public are allowed in and gather round like vultures.*
- ▶ *Don't forget an umbrella, a warm jacket, sandwiches and a thermos of coffee.*
- ▶ *Take lots of change in a container with a lid and when you've acquired a few notes, lock them in a separate bag in the car.*
- ▶ *Share the space with a friend or take a helper so you have a chance to walk round the site yourself, take a toilet break, and see what else is on offer but don't buy unless you see something you've been planning to get anyway. What's the point of de-cluttering your own home and then filling it up with someone else's clutter?*

Insight

If you want to hold a sale in your own garage, get a friend or family member to help you. It's much easier to cope with any unexpected situation that might arise.

SELLING EXPENSIVE ITEMS

▶ *Sell some large item you never use: your old motorbike; the children's outgrown pedal bikes; the exercise bike or rowing equipment you've relegated to the basement. These could bring you in a small but worthwhile amount if you sell through a dealer, advertise in your local newspaper or a specialist magazine or online.*

▶ *If you have a second car you don't really need, selling it will not only bring in some money but save you in maintenance costs and insurance.*

▶ *Sell that expensive dinner service you inherited that sits gathering dust and is never used. Some auctioneers have open days when you can get antique objects valued. You can then decide whether it's worth selling or not.*

SELLING OUTGROWN CLOTHES

▶ *Have you got outgrown school clothes that some younger child could use? Sell them at a knock-down price to parents with younger children – they get a bargain and you get a little cash.*

▶ *Have you got expensive clothes in good condition you are not likely to wear again such as an outgrown party dress or wedding outfit? Take them to an upmarket dress agency or seconds shop where they may be taken on a sale-or-return basis.*

PARTY SELLING

Insight

Party selling is best for people who are naturally gregarious and outgoing and have plenty of friends and acquaintances (preferably with a little money to spend).

Giving a selling party at home can be a fun way to earn a little money and entertain friends and acquaintances. You can either make products yourself and then sell them, say three weeks before

Christmas when people are looking for interesting presents, or sign up with a company selling specific products in which you will probably get help with planning and organizing the party and a certain number of discounted or possibly free products, depending on how much you manage to sell at your party.

Party plan companies can offer anything from fashion, lingerie, shoes, handbags, children's books, jewellery, beauty products, toiletries and candles. If you make things yourself these can vary from greetings cards, candles, pottery, knitted garments, soft toys or other crafts. Whatever the products are, make sure they are either exclusive or competitively priced. Entry should be by invitation not advertisement.

Questions the thrifty should get answered before signing up with any company include the following: What is the commission (discount)? How do you get paid (some companies allow you to keep the money you have made, others require you to send it all to them and write you a cheque later)? Is there a money-back guarantee? Can you just sign up for one party or will you be expected to hold regular parties? What sort of training and support does the company offer, if any, and do they charge for these? What are the start up costs and what to you get in your starter kit? Do you like the products – it's very difficult to sell anything you're not in sympathy with.

SELLING ONLINE

▶ *You can sell anything on eBay from old junk from the attic to books, bicycles, and slide projectors. Start off with things that are not worth much until you get a feel for it and remember that if you sell too much you will need to register as a trader with the tax man.*

▶ *Amazon Marketplace is a good place to sell videos, books and CDs. Like eBay it's easy to sign up for but make sure your descriptions of the goods are accurate and package items up carefully when it comes to sending them to buyers.*

MAKE THE MOST OF A SKILL

▸ *Are you a knitter, embroiderer, potter or woodworker? Do you make handmade papers, soft toys, creations out of papier maché or attractive cushion covers? Why not sell items you make? Depending on your output and competence, you could sell items by word of mouth, at Christmas bazaars, to local retail shops, at local craft shows or on the internet.*

▸ *Teach others how to make things. This can be done at home or in the local school, community centre or church hall. If necessary take a teaching course yourself first to give you confidence.*

▸ *Make money from your own website. This is difficult and takes a lot of work and may not be successful. It's vital to get listed on the main search engines and your website itself will cost something and needs to be well-designed, kept up to date and you must be able to fulfil orders.*

▸ *If you are a good and experienced cook, advertise your services as a personal chef, perhaps to provide finger foods for company seminars or to go into someone's kitchen and cook dinner for 12 people. Cooking can be fitted in to other commitments and you only need take as many jobs as you can manage. Obviously you need experience in catering for largish numbers and to know the catering regulations.*

MAKING THE MOST OF EXTRA SPACE IN YOUR HOME

Insight

Don't underestimate yourself. You might be surprised to find how many things you can do that people will pay for. For example, word processing or filing for people working from home, bookkeeping, gardening or ironing.

▸ *If you have a spare room consider renting it to foreign students who need somewhere to live for a few months while they learn English. Enquire in local language colleges. This gives you the opportunity between lettings to put up friends or family who come to stay. But, be warned, you will be taxed on such earnings.*

▶ *If you have a spare room with ensuite bath or shower facilities, offer it as a B&B. If you are gregarious and prepared always to be there for breakfast you can meet interesting people in this way and earn a tidy amount.*

Occasional and part-time jobs

One of the benefits of a part-time job is that a couple of evening shifts here or there leaves you plenty of time to study or do other things. Popular part-time jobs include bar work, promotions, hotel work, retail jobs (working in shops, petrol stations and so on) and working with recruitment agencies. Don't dismiss part-time work because you think it won't pay enough. What seems like a pittance may make the difference between debt or survival. After all, while you're working, you can't be spending. Part-time workers have the same legal rights as full-timers. This means that no employer can discriminate against you for only working a few hours a week. Check in the job description for entitlements such as holiday pay, sick pay, bonuses and other perks. Part-time jobs such as bar work or being a waiter often earn more than a basic hourly wage, particularly taking into account tips and bonuses and maybe food and drink whilst on or after your shift. Consider the whole package as well as associated benefits and disadvantages. Factors like distance to work, flexibility of hours and work environment can all make a huge difference. A part-time job that is both enjoyable and suits your own schedule may not pay as much as others – but because of these plus points, may be the best choice.

Insight

Many of the opportunities suggested here will require extra training, which can be taken as part-time or intensive courses. There may be local courses to help acquire skills or brush up on existing skills.

▶ *Do you practise yoga? Become a yoga teacher and take classes locally in local adult education colleges, schools, community centres or churches. Offer your yoga classes to local businesses who may provide space for after-work sessions.*

▶ *Pose as a model for art colleges or artists. This can be boring and tiring and you have to be patient and able to sit still but you don't have to be beautiful or have a fantastic figure and good models are in demand, so contact your local university, college or art society.*

▶ *Various interesting opportunities exist if you are a skilled and careful driver. You will need the relevant licences depending on what sort of vehicle you are prepared to drive and may have to take an aptitude test. You can deliver new cars or even buses, ambulances and luxury limousines to dealers or new owners. There are many full-time drivers delivering cars but extra drivers are often needed during the summer.*

▶ *Become an in-store demonstrator. You need to be confident and able to talk in front of people easily. You might be required to hold food-tasting sessions or demonstrate a new kitchen gadget in a supermarket or department store.*

▶ *For 12–24 days in June, during the Wimbledon Championships, drivers are needed to chauffeur players, officials and VIPs to and from the Championships in and around London. It doesn't pay much but a uniform and light meals are provided and you get the chance to meet interesting people and watch the matches.*

▶ *Some companies offer various incentives, vouchers and sometimes cash for taking part in a survey. You won't become rich but may make a little pocket money and receive the occasional free gift. Several websites offer incentives for taking part in surveys. You might get the chance to win an iPod or vouchers for weekend breaks or to spend at places like Ikea or Amazon. You will have to fill in all your details but if you don't mind doing that, why not?*

▶ *Become a personal assistant. Many people who work from home need someone to organize their lives from scheduling appointments, meeting repairmen, picking up laundry, making travel plans, organizing events and generally leaving your client free to get on with their job. If you are a well-organized person and particularly if you have secretarial or accountancy* skills, this is a way of making a living. You can decide how much time you are prepared to give. You can join an agency or advertise your skills in the local paper.

▶ If you have a good telephone manner, telesales can earn money quickly. Call centres cope with such things as customer service support or active selling. Although the work may be pressured and you may be monitored, the rewards can be good, with high basic rates and in some sectors, very good commission. Summer jobs like telesales or call centre work have high turnover rates so are fairly readily available. Many call centres are open 24 hours a day so there is plenty of night work which is usually much better pay than day work.

▶ In summer, particularly in tourist areas, people shop more, staff go on holiday, shops open later and some even have 24 hour opening so extra staff are often required. Summer jobs can also be found in out-of-town stores and retail parks, which have more trouble recruiting people due to their location. Many students start working part-time in shops and other businesses and find that they can progress to full time in the holidays. Once you have been trained and are competent many companies will look to keep you and use the skills that you have acquired – even if it means you only work a few months during your holidays. Christmas holidays are also particularly busy times with longer opening hours so extra staff are often required.

▶ One of the best places to find factory work opportunities is your local paper, or alternatively, your local recruitment agency. This may not be a favourite, but with work readily available, it provides lots of summer job opportunities. Much of the work is unskilled and requires little or no previous experience. The pay can vary tremendously, as can the hours available.

▶ Become a film extra. Register with a casting agent or check in your local newspaper for any TV shows or movies being filmed in your area. You may be called upon at a moment's notice and spend most of the day hanging around and you certainly won't meet the stars but you can earn a useful day's wage with bonuses for things like providing your own *costume or doing a 'walk-on'. It is illegal for an agent to charge up-front fees but online agencies will usually ask for a subscription fee.*

▶ *Become a lifeguard in an apartment block with a swimming pool. If you have a certificates in lifesaving, CPR and first-aid, apply to apartment management companies*

Student holiday jobs

There are various opportunities for students who need either part-time work while studying or job opportunities during vacation times. A full-time holiday job will pay a weekly or monthly wage which could work out better than an hourly part-time job rate. Before you start work, find out from your employer how the tax issue is going to be resolved. At worst you may get it deducted from your wages, but then you should be able to claim it back at the end of the tax year. Recruitment agencies provide short- or longer-term cover in a huge range of industries. Much agency work is available in peak holiday seasons, including the summer, when many full-time workers are keen to take time off, leaving businesses under-staffed.

There are many opportunities for students to work at home (see 'Occasional and part-time jobs' on p. 249) or abroad, for example as counsellors or support staff on summer camps for children. If you have a sports skill (anything from rock climbing to archery or horse-riding), or if you have social work skills or first-aid skills you might be taken on as a counsellor, otherwise you could find yourself working in the kitchen. The Work and Travel USA programme offers jobs in amusement parks, food and beverage retail concessions, retail stores and shops in tourist towns, national parks and ski resorts as well as jobs as lifeguards, housekeepers or maids, decorators, landscapers or janitors. You won't earn much money, probably just your keep but you will have a chance to see a different side of life and meet people. A useful website is www.globalchoices.co.uk.

TEN THRIFTY EARNING TIPS

1 *If you'd like to take on regular babysitting, try and go on a short course, get a certificate in cardiopulmonary resuscitation (CPR) and in babysitting itself if you can find courses locally.*

2 *You may not be paid for house-sitting itself but you could get paid a small amount for tending the garden or seeing to other tasks around the house while you are there.*

3 *Clean and repair old furniture you intend taking to a car boot sale and display it attractively. You're much more likely to sell something that looks good than a heap of old bits and pieces.*

4 *Party selling can be an entertaining way to earn some money but make sure the company you are dealing with is bona fide, ask all the right questions first and don't sign up with any company you have doubts about.*

5 *If you have expensive clothes you never wear, take them along to a dress agency rather than to a charity shop or second-hand clothes shop and hope to get back at least a percentage of what you paid in the first place.*

6 *Make something of your ability to create mouth-watering cakes or scented candles and sell them through the local paper or through a local shop.*

7 *There are opportunities to be an artists' model. Local art groups and art colleges are often looking for models because it is not a particularly glamorous job and can be boring and uncomfortable. You don't need to be beautiful – in fact an interesting face and figure is usually more sought after than perfection.*

8 *Become an extra. You won't earn a lot but you do meet other people and find out how movies are made.*

9   *If you are a student, sign up for a summer holiday job in an adventure holiday centre or summer camp. It won't make you a fortune but is a way to discover a different part of the world with free board and lodging. If you have a sports skill, you can practise that too.*

10 *Take part in a survey. There are many online surveys which are not too exacting to fill in and you may be rewarded with free products or a cash bonus.*

QUICK REVISION TEST

1 *If you trade on eBay, how soon should you register your trading activities to the tax authorities?*

2 *What is a home-sitting agency likely to require before accepting you on their list?*

3 *What products can you offer if you want to organize a party-selling evening?*

4 *What are your rights as a part-timer as opposed to a full-time worker?*

5 *What qualities do you need to be a telesales operator?*

Answers to the quick revision tests

1 Getting the thrifty habit

1 *To regularly and consistently save unnecessary expenditure so that you control your money and can achieve specific goals.*

2 *Plan your spending for the coming week; leave your credit cards at home; take a packed lunch to work; give the children something absorbing to do at home; give up smoking; drink tap water.*

3 *Read a specialist magazine on the product in question; find online reviews of the product, go to your nearest store and ask advice from an assistant; ask if you can have a demonstration and test the product; join a consumer organization and ask its advice.*

4 *Open a high-interest savings account; put all loose change into a piggy bank.*

5 *Not getting into debt in the first place.*

2 Know your shopping rights

1 *That they should be of 'satisfactory quality', 'fit for purpose', and 'as described'.*

2 *Seven days in the UK; three days in the USA.*

3 *The retailer or trader.*

4 *Have a note of what you want to say; all receipts and other documents; the name of the person you wish to speak to; your reference number, agreement or account number.*

5 *Your local objective advice organization such as the local Citizens Advice Bureau or the local authority advisory service (if there is one).*

3 Thrifty money matters

1 *Wage/salary; income from savings and investments; any benefits; maintenance; contributions from family or lodger.*
2 *For example: housekeeping; rent or mortgage; all insurance expenses; income tax; local taxes; fuel and water; telephone; travel expenses; childcare; TV licence; clothes; entertaining; medical expenses; caring; savings; newspapers; loan repayments.*
3 *A secured loan uses your home as security.*
4 *A mortgage broker.*
5 *Objective advisors such as the Citizens Advice Bureau or the Debt Advice Trust.*
6 *Rent, mortgage, car, telephone, home maintenance, lights, heating.*

4 Beat the bills

1 *Get organized with filing and folders for individual categories of correspondence.*
2 *Draught-proof your home.*
3 *They use less energy and last longer.*
4 *A low-flow showerhead will reduce the use of water and electricity.*
5 *Reflect the heat from a radiator with aluminium sheet; hang a large rug over a wall; line a wall with bookshelves; fix wooden panelling to a wall; put up textured wall coverings such as felt or hessian.*

5 Internet know-how

1 *Not unless you need the newest technology. Last year's model will be cheaper and do everything most people need.*
2 *Sleep mode powers down the computer so that it uses 70 per cent less power than if you leave it on.*

3 *This may well be a spam message, which can be used to spread a virus. Delete it at once without opening it.*

4 *.gov and .org (e.g. www.herbsociety.org.uk).*

5 *If someone uses your credit card fraudulently, you can cancel the payment and the card issuer has to refund you.*

---

6 The fine art of haggling

1 *Valuable items such as gold, jewellery, carpets and furniture.*

2 *You can often get discounts on the cost of staying in a hotel even if there are set prices. Try and arrange to stay out of season or during the week rather than at weekends.*

3 *With expensive equipment such as a digital camera or a computer package, ask for extra accessories to be added to the deal, such as a carrying case, extra batteries or a free warranty.*

4 *Shop late when traders are starting to pack up; start to walk away as though losing interest; offer to buy three or four objects at a discount; offer cash-in-hand; establish a rapport with the vendor; be patient; always be prepared to walk away empty-handed if the price isn't right.*

5 *Don't try to haggle over bus or train tickets, bottled water, alcohol or groceries.*

---

7 Thrifty shopping

1 *The interest rate on most store cards is extremely high.*

2 *Tax concessions mean that charity shops are often able to sell items more cheaply.*

3 *Even if there's a notice saying all breakages must be paid for, if you can prove the item was broken because it was badly placed or poorly stacked or otherwise not caused by your own negligence you should not have to pay.*

4 *Excellently priced, really warm and sturdy outdoor wear from jackets and anoraks to boots, hats and gloves.*

5 *Just after Christmas.*

8 Reduce, reuse and recycle

1 *Bottles, jars, tumblers, wine glasses, coloured gravel, aggregate in road building, in golf bunkers.*
2 *Reduce, Reuse, Recycle.*
3 *Put on the compost heap; turn it into papier maché; as storage boxes.*
4 *Take to a local pharmacy.*
5 *Bamboo, grass, straw, rubber, cork, cellulose (from newspaper), sorghum, coconut palm wood.*

9 Savings on clothes

1 *Keep hanging clothes in plastic zipper bags; keep clothes clean; hang a bunch of bay leaves or a few drops of lavender oil on a cloth in the clothes cupboard or place a muslin bag of ground cloves, cinnamon, black pepper and orris root amongst the clothes.*
2 *Cotton, silk, wool, linen, viscose, bamboo, hemp.*
3 *January for things like sheets, pillowcases, blankets, quilts, table linen.*
4 *Large supermarket chains, or cheap fashion stores such as T K Maxx, New Look, Matalan, Primark, Kmart, Walmart.*
5 *Rub the suede gently with an emery board then hold the suede over the steam from a kettle.*

10 Saving money on food and drink

1 *Crisps and sweet snacks; frozen meals; value-added products such as canned tomatoes with herbs; ready-grated cheese; pre-washed vegetables.*
2 *Fruit juice; baby wipes; skimmed milk powder; pulses; ice cream; frozen vegetables.*

3 *Pour it into ice cube trays and freeze it to use later when cooking sauces and stews.*

4 *Wholemeal grains are more filling and you therefore need less of them.*

5 *Putting food that has reached simmering point in a saucepan into an insulated casserole dish, allowing the contents to cook in its own heat for several hours.*

11 Thrift in the home

1 *Removing hard water deposits; cleaning windows; cleaning the toilet; cleaning glass tabletops; (with grated potato or tea leaves) for cleaning vases and decanters.*

2 *Laid on trestles as a table; fitted into a frame to make a bed.*

3 *Make cheap café curtains; make a party dress for a small child.*

4 *Send them by email or make your own.*

5 *Take them to the public library; give them a dressing-up box of old clothes; provide a craft box with scissors, glues and collected cards, buttons, sequins and varied haberdashery.*

12 Economical transport

1 *A car powered by electricity and petrol; the petrol provides extra power when required. Cleaner than petrol or diesel and more efficient.*

2 *Maintain an even speed; buy a diesel car if you take frequent, short journeys; get your tyres checked regularly; don't go over 60 mph (100 kph) on motorways; remove all roof storage when not in use.*

3 *Lightweight; comfortable; free on public transport; high resale value; more thief proof than traditional bikes.*

4 *Coach or bus.*

5 *Own a small car; take an advanced driving course; have off-street parking; belong to a large motoring organization.*

13 Thrifty leisure time and holidays

1 *Free browsing and borrowing; time on a computer; comfortable chairs; story readings for children.*
2 *Lunchtime concerts, TV and radio recordings of popular programmes; meet-the-author evenings at bookshops or libraries.*
3 *Find a co-operating hotel; get the right credit card; fly at the times of year when airlines are offering extra air miles; pick the right airport.*
4 *Book a room in a suite hotel; go camping; book a hotel which is free for children up to 16 years; look for theme park restaurants where children eat free.*
5 *Big Apple Greeter and a free cruise on the Staten Island ferry in New York; buskers and other entertainers in Covent Garden or go kite-flying on Hampstead Heath in London; join a free city tour in Singapore; take a bike ride in Copenhagen; hop on a City Circle tram in Melbourne.*

14 Make the most of the garden

1 *Cooked food; dairy products; nappies; shiny paper; droppings from meat-eating animals; magazines; coal ash, diseased plants; roots of persistent plants; synthetic fabrics; glass; metal.*
2 *Lay them over a fallow bed to keep the weeds down; as a 'lid' on the compost heap to conserve heat and moisture.*
3 *Install a water butt; water generously but only once a week; water early in the morning or late at night; grow plants that will not need watering; use plastic bottles for irrigating individual plants; lay a seep hose near the roots of plants; mulch round established plants to prevent the soil from drying out; add absorbent granules to your potting compost.*
4 *They are good on the compost heap; make an excellent liquid fertilizer; can be eaten as soup or turned into wine or beer.*
5 *They are flexible and strong so useful as plant ties or gate hinges.*

15 Earn a little something

1 *Within three months of starting to trade.*
2 *Experience with animals; a computer, printer and internet connection; mobile phone; willingness to go for walks in all weathers; willingness to sign up for six months.*
3 *Almost anything, from things you have made yourself to products provided by a party-selling company which might range from handbags and clothes to children's books, candles or beauty products.*
4 *Part-timers have the same rights as full-time workers. So an employer cannot discriminate against you for only working a few days a week.*
5 *You need a good telephone manner and the ability to work under pressure.*

Taking it further

Useful contacts

CONSUMER ADVICE

In the UK:

Citizens Advice Bureaux (CAB), www.citizensadvice.org.uk:
Run local free advice centres; look in the phone book or visit the
website.

Consumer Direct, www.consumerdirect.gov.uk, 0845 404 0506:
Government-funded telephone and online service offering
information and advice on consumer issues.

Consumer's Association, Which? Castlemead, Gascoyne Way,
Hertford, SG14 1LH, www.which.co.uk, 01992 822800:
Membership organization that tests products and gives consumer
information and advice to members.

Department for Business, Innovation and Skills (formerly DTI),
www.berr.gov.uk: Information on consumer law.

Department for Work and Pensions, www.dwp.gov.uk:
Information on such benefits as Cold Weather Payment.

Consumer Focus, www.consumerfocus.org.uk, statutory
organization campaigning for a fair deal for consumers in England,
Wales, and Scotland and for postal services in Northern Ireland
(individual enquirers go to Consumer Direct (see above).

In the USA:

Consumer Federation of America (CFA), 1620, 1 St, Suite 200, Washington, DC 20006, www.consumerfed.org: Consumer advice and educational organization on telephone services, insurance and financial services, product safety, healthcare etc.

Consumer Union, 101 Truman Avenue, Yonkers, NY 10703–1057, www.consumersunion.org: Independent, non-profits testing on products, services, personal finance, health and nutrition. Sells consumer reports.

Federal Citizen Information Center, www.consumeraction.gov: Produce a free Consumer Action Handbook – a guide to buying a car or home, preventing identity theft, understanding credit and resolving problems after a purchase.

Federal Trade Commission, www.ftc.gov: Advice for consumers.

MONEY

In the UK:

Citizens Advice Bureaux (CAB) (see under 'Consumer advice')

Financial Services Authority (FSA), www.moneymadeclear.fsa.gov.uk, 0300 500 5000 : Consumer helpline, gives general information but can't investigate individual complaints.

To find an independent financial adviser use www.unbiased.co.uk.

In the USA:

Consumer Action, 221 Main St. Ste. 480, San Francisco, CA 94105; 523 West Sixth Street. Suite 1105, Los Angeles, CA 90014; PO Box 1762, Washington, DC 20013; www.consumeraction.gov: Educational and advice organization specializing in credit, finance and telecommunications.

Federal Reserve Board, www.federalreserve.gov/consumerinfo: Website has information and advice for consumers on many financial subjects.

ENERGY EFFICIENCY

In the UK:

Energy Saving Trust, 21 Dartmouth Street, London, SW1H 9BP, www.energysavingtrust.org.uk, 0800 512 012 (helpline): Free, independent and local energy-saving advice with local advice centres.

The National Energy Foundation, Davy Avenue, Kowlhill, Milton Keynes, MK5 8NG, www.nef.org.uk, 01908 665555: Website has detailed advice on saving energy.

In the USA:

Alliance to Save Energy, www.ase.org: A non-profit coalition of business, government, environmental and consumer leaders who promote the efficient and clean use of energy worldwide. Offers energy efficiency tips and resources on its website.

US Department of Energy, 1000 Independence Avenue, SW Washington, DC 20585, www.energy.gov: Information on tax credits for energy efficiency in your home and car.

COMPUTER/ONLINE

Aidis Trust, 3 Gunthorpe Street, London E1 7RQ, www.aidis.org, 0845 120 3719: Website has information for disabled people on using computers, which internet provider to choose and internet safety guidelines.

Citizens Advice Bureau (CAB) (see under 'Consumer advice').

Consumer Direct (see under 'Consumer advice').

Trading Standards Institute, www.tradingstandards.gov.uk: Advice on shopping on the internet with advice leaflets online.

Zyra, www.zyra.org.uk: A wealth of information and advice on any subject under the sun including computers and computing.

SHOPPING

In the UK:

The Consumer's Association (see under 'Consumer advice').

Emmaus, www.emmaus.org.uk, general enquiries 01223 576 103: Contact your nearest branch to find second-hand furniture outlets.

Good Deal Directory, www.gooddealdirectory.co.uk: Directory of designer showrooms and factory shops in the UK.

Shopping Villages, www.shoppingvillages.com: A guide to shopping villages, outlet villages, outlet stores, factory shops and factory outlets in the UK.

Official Great British Factory Shop guide by Gillian Cuttress, available from Amazon, www.factoryshopguide.com.

Glasses Direct, Unit 2, Charlton Business Park, Crudwell Road, Malmesbury, Wiltshire, SN16 9RU, www.glassesdirect.co.uk, 0845 688 2020. Provide cheap prescription spectacles.

Spex 4 Less, 552 Chorley Old Road, Bolton, BL1 6AB, www.spex4less.com, 0151 632 6611 Offers cheap frames for prescription glasses.

In the USA:

Emmaus, www.emmaus-international.org: Contact your nearest branch to find second-hand furniture outlets.

Real Outlets, www.realoutlets.com: A list of all factory stores and outlet centres in the USA.

Outlet Bound, www.outletbound.com: A guide to discount outlets throughout the USA by location, store name, US map, category or brand name.

In France:

Roubaix/Tourcoing, north of Lille, has the largest conglomeration of factory and discount shops in the north of France.

Troyes has two large factory shopping centres on the RN71 towards Dijon (Marques Avenue and McArthur Glen).

Reims has a Marques City and a McArthur Glen where Villeroy & Boch and Black and Decker both have outlets.

RECYCLING

In the UK:

Mail Preference Service, www.mpsonline.org.uk, 020 7291 3310: For stopping unwanted mail coming through your letter box.

Save a Cup Scheme, Suite 2, Bridge House, Bridge Street, High Wycombe, HP11 2EL: Information on recycling the millions of hard-wall polystyrene cups used in the UK every week.

The Curtain Exchange, www.thecurtainexchange.net: Offers an extensive range of bespoke and ready-made curtains and blinds, as well as a second-hand curtain service.

The Real Nappy Campaign, www.goreal.org.uk.

The Real Nappy Project, The Create Centre, Smeaton Road, Bristol, BS1 6XN, www.recyclingconsortium.org.uk, 0117 914 3450. Encourages people to use washable nappies, information on how to use and where to find them.

Tools for Self Reliance, Southampton, Hants, So40 7GY, www.tfsr.org, supports small businesses in Africa with refurbished tools.

Oxfam Bring Bring Scheme, Freepost, LON 16281, London WC1 3BR, www.Oxfam.org.uk: Encourages and accepts collections of old mobile phones for recycling.

National Association of Toy and Leisure Libraries, www.natll.org.uk: Community resources for play which may include equipment, toys for loan, dedicated space and skilled staff.

In the USA:

Recycle Appeal USA, Suite 260, 5600 Oakbrook Parkway, Norcross, GA 30093, USA, www.recyclingappealusa.com: Encourages community organized recycling of old printer cartridges, cell phones, personal digital assistants (PDAs) and blackberries – can organize postage-paid envelopes or free pick-ups.

Lions Clubs in the USA and Australia, www.lionsclubs.org: Local clubs collect eye glasses for recycling.

USA Toy Libraries Association, 1326 Wilmette Avenue, Wilmette, IL 60091, usatla.org: Has a network of toy libraries throughout the USA.

CLOTHES

In the UK:

Designer Warehouse Sales, 5-6 Islington Studios, Thane Works, Thane Villas, London N7 7NU; 020 7697 9888. Hold 12 sales a year of designer clothes at low prices.

MacCulloch & Wallis, 25 Dering Street, London W1M 5DJ, www.macculloch-wallis.co.uk: Fabrics and haberdashery galore.

In the USA:

Silk Traders, www.silktraders.com: A website linking to several firms offering discount dress and upholstery fabrics.

FOOD

In the UK:

Lakeland, Alexandra Buildings, Windermere, Cumbria, UK, LA23 1BQ, www.lakeland.co.uk, 015394 88100: Catalogue has storage boxes and bags for food of all types.

Farmer's Markets UK Directory, www.farmersmarket.net: Lists farmer's markets throughout the UK.

THE HOME

In the UK:

Learn Direct, Dearing House, 1 Young Street, Sheffield, S1 4UP, www.learndirect.co.uk, helpline 0800 101 901: Gives advice and runs courses throughout the UK.

Home Learning College, First Floor 221-241 Beckenham Road, Beckenham, Kent BR3 4UF, www.homelearningcollege.com, 0800 912 2926: Advise and run courses leading to qualifications in computers, bookkeeping, marketing and other business skills.

Lakeland (see under 'Food').

MPS Mailing Preference Services (see under 'Recycle').

Telephone Preference Service Ltd., 5th floor, Haymarket House, 1 Oxenden Street, London, SW1Y 4EE, www.tpsonline.org.uk; 020 7291 3320: Will stop unwanted telephone calls to your home by sales people.

National Association of Toy and Leisure Libraries,
www.natll.org.uk. 020 7755 4600.

In the USA:

Telephone Preference Service, PO Box 9008, Farningdale, NY
11735–9008: Will put a stop to junk phone calls.

TRANSPORT

In the UK:

The Automobile Association (AA), Member Administration,
Contact Centre, Lambert House, Stockport Road, Cheadle,
SK8 2DY, www.theaa.com, 0161 488 7544. The UK's largest
breakdown organization.

In the USA:

Alliance to Save Energy, www.ase.org: A non-profit coalition of
business, government, environmental and consumer leaders who
promote the efficient and clean use of energy worldwide. Offers
energy efficiency tips and resources on its website.

The American Automobile Association (AAA), www.aaa.com,
800/222-4357: The country's largest auto club supplying its
members with maps, insurance and emergency road service. If
you are a member of a foreign automobile club with reciprocal
arrangements you can get free AAA services in America.

US Department of Energy Efficiency and Renewable Energy.
1000 Independence Avenue, SW Washington, DC 20585,
www.eere.energy.gov: Information on tax credits for energy
efficiency in your home and car.

In the UK:

Euro Tunnel, www.eurotunnel.com, 08443 353535: For recorded information.

National Express Ltd, 08457 225 333, www.nationalexpress.com.

Ferry travel, www.ferryto.co.uk; www.eurodrive.co.uk and www.seat61.com: These are three search engines that claim to find the cheapest ferry from England to places on the continent.

Car rentals, www.carrentals.co.uk: Will search up to 40 car hire suppliers to find the best deal in many countries.

Discount holidays, www.holidaydiscountcentre.net: Will search for discount holidays for you.

Eurodrive Networks Ltd, Image House, Station Road, Tottenham Hale, London, N17 9LR. www.eurodrive.co.uk, 0844 371 8021. Self drive travel agent with online press comparison and family booking website.

The Man in Seat 61, www.seat61.com. Information on travelling by train and ship to Europe and beyond.

European Health Insurance Card: Dept of Health, www.ehic.org; PO Box 1114, Newcastle upon Tyne, NE99 2TL; 0845 605 0707.

Amtrak, www.amtrak.com. Provides an intercity passenger train service throughout the USA and to Canada.

Greyhound Lines Inc, www.greyhound.com, 1-800-231-2222.

Corniche Events, Hoppingwood Farm, Robin Hood Way, London, SW20 OAB, www.corniche-events.com: For driving jobs during Wimbledon fortnight.

Employment4students, Highlands House, 165 The Broadway, Wimbledon, SW19 1NE, www.e4s.co.uk, 0845 094 1832: Finds part-time employment for students.

www.ukparttimejobs.co.uk: Online site for holiday jobs all over the world.

www.actorsandextras.co.uk; 01329 848142 (UK): Agency which may be able to offer jobs as extras.

www.moviex.com (USA): Agency which may be able to offer jobs as extras.

Index